# My Angel And Me

www.bodymindspiritnews.com

By
Charlie R. Brown

*Copyright © 2001 by Charlie R. Brown First Printing*
*Copyright © 2005 by Charlie R. Brown Second Printing*
*Copyright © 2007 by Charlie R. Brown Third Printing*

*All rights reserved. No part of this work may be reproduced or used in any form without express written permission from the copyright holder.*

*Edited by: Sandra Beaver*
*www.authoreasy.com*

First Printing © 2001
Heflin Printing Center, Toledo, Ohio

Second Printing, © 2005
Edited by Sandra Beaver
Awareness Publishing Company, LLC

Third Printing, © 2007
Edited and published by Sandra Beaver
www.authoreasy.com

ISBN# 978-0-6151-7754-0

Library of Congress Control Number #2002107108

For additional stories and articles of inspiration and food for thought, visit us online at

**www.bodymindspiritnews.com**

*Cover by: Mother Nature*

# Foreword

If I were asked to suggest a book to someone looking for a variety of subjects about the spiritual and psychic realm, I would suggest *My Angel and Me*.

Although I am fairly well versed on spiritual and metaphysical subjects and a little of my knowledge is shared in this book, I learned even more as I read through the pages. I met Charlie Brown several years ago at the spiritualist church that I belong to. I must say that when I mention his name, I get a few chuckles from my friends about the cartoon character. Even though Charlie and his Pisces personality and his book are of a very serious nature, there is a part in it about him and his brother and Madison Avenue. As I read about it, I laughed so hard that I had tears running down my cheeks. It would not be a laughing matter to some people because it is of hard knocks, but the way Charlie put it on paper reminded me of some of my trials in life. Laughter is a way that I learned, with a friend of mine, how to deal with hard times. It was the highlight of the book for me, because it reminded me that no matter how bad things seem, laughing and faith is more healing and helpful with finding solutions than being depressed and sad. So without knowing as he was writing it, he brought a huge dose of healing to me. I think laughter is music for the soul and is a great healing tool.

You might ask what is an angel or a guide. I think you will see in the pages of the book that they are helpers from the spirit world that have helped Charlie and many of us who have welcomed their help and knowledge to progress in a more spiritual way of growing and learning. Because Charlie chose to let his angels-guides in to work with him, he has become very well learned in many aspects of the metaphysical world.

He is a very good psychic medium, healer, and teacher, who through his guides can channel these energies from the other side to this side. I have learned over the years that Charlie has a real God given gift, and he shares some of his knowledge about his abilities and his angels in this book. I am sure you will see he has many talents, and you will be as happy as I am that he chose to share this information with us. Enjoy reading.

Many Blessings,
Judith Pleasant
Toledo Author

# Dedicated to

**LYLE E. BROWN**
Nancy Scharf
Sharon Bendix
David Laing
Barbara Munroe
Rocco T. Pizza
Rev. Margaret Schmidt
And all the Healing Ministers at the
**U.C.S.S. SPIRITUAL CENTER**
102 Aspen Avenue
Orange City, FL
Chartered under the International General Assembly
of Spiritualists, Ashtabula, Ohio

*Keep the Faith and Pass It Along...*

My Angel and Me, Registered in the Library of Congress
*#2002107108*

# ABOUT THE COVER
## A pencil and ink drawing by
## MOTHER NATURE

This is a psychic artist's concept of my spirit guide, "Flaming Arrow." He is a hunter and protective guide.

The artist, Mother Nature, has beautifully captured the balance of the universe between the earth and sky, mother earth and father sun, and the union of man, animals, and the masters of the sky.

The wolf is not only protection, but intuitiveness as well. The eagle looks ahead into the future while helping us avoid the stumbling blocks of the past.

The light of wisdom, the light and understanding of the universe surround the trio.

# INDEX

Page 1..................................................I Felt My Brother Die
Page 6...................Heart Patient Watches Own Botched By-Pass
Page 9.........................................The Curse of Madison Avenue
Page 21.................................................Physician Heal Thyself
Page 26.......................Ancient Lady Saves Newspaper Office
Page 29...............................................Psychics of Substance
Page 34..............................................Return To Our Roots
Page 37.........................................The Art of Wishful Thinking
Page 41......................................Two Seconds From Eternity
Page 44................................... To Pray or Not to Pray
Page 48................................................. My Dog the Psychic
Page 52................................................... Sun Worship
Page 54...............................................The Realm of Possibility
Page 57.............................................. The Doctor Within
Page 61.................................................... The Last Cry
Page 65.................................... The Euphoria of Salvation
Page 68............................. 2012 – A Mayan Transformation
Page 71..............................The Faith of a Grain of Mustard
Page 75...............Sticks and Stones Does Not a Friendship Break
Page 78...........................................................Hell on Earth
Page 82...............................................The Law of Three
Page 89........................... Deadly Fiery Message from the Grave
Page 93...........................................................Psychometry
Page 98................Growth, Physically, Emotionally, Spiritually
Page 102...........................Ancient Lady Defies Tornado
Page 106......................... Trappings of a Psychic Vampire

vii

# I FELT MY BROTHER DIE

It was early April, 1976, that I first became conscious of my dreams and the aches throughout my body that accompanied them each time I awoke. It was as though someone or something had been pulling on every muscle in my body throughout the night. I had been studying phenomena for the past decade but had never accepted dreams as a method of communication. It was this awakening that prompted my search for an expert and some acceptable answers. It was an endless search but one, which I knew, would be rewarding.

I soon learned that some dreams were of a psychic nature, while others were merely wishful thinking or daily stress and strain releasing itself. The most remarkable dreams were those of an educational structure as though coming from a classroom. I remembered one dream involving dogs and cats, and a teacher who called himself "Orr" was instructing me. He was lecturing on the mentality of humans on a balance scale with dogs and cats. The point he was making is that animals can see energy emanating from other animals or people, and *feel* it.

I couldn't understand the point of the dream until I attended a workshop by Carol Ann Liaros. Carol, a foremost authority in the field, fully convinced me and helped me to understand the lectures my teacher had been giving me for some time. Instead of dismissing them as another stupid dream, I began taking notes and evaluating each one. At this time, I had been living in Ohio for nine years and had seen my brother once during this length of time. I had almost erased him from my mind, as we were never really as close as brothers should be. I suppose that was because he always needed help, and I was either unable or refused to give it.

The past six weeks had brought nothing but vague dreams of him. Each morning when I awoke, I had severe headaches and pains around my heart and my limbs. I had been studying the positive and negative energy fields and how they could be consciously directed toward another person. After a lengthy meditation, I became keenly aware of a projection pattern coming from a former acquaintance. At the end of my meditation, all the pain had left.

The next few nights brought strange dreams of my hometown in Alabama. I tried furiously to come up with even a minute link, but each attempt brought nothing but frustration. Exactly nine days later, I awoke with the strongest urge to return to Alabama. Making another common mistake in the psychic world, I began rationalizing and attributed the dreams to homesickness.

The next five days, the urge became more defined. The following Thursday, when I took off from work for lunch, I drove straight to the turnpike and headed for Alabama. After driving about ten hours, I began experiencing breathing difficulties, and my heart began pounding as though it would burst. By this time, it was almost dark. I pulled into a gas station in a small berg near Chattanooga.

I went into the restaurant after splashing cold water on my face near the gas pump. I sat down and looked for a waitress. I was distracted by an image entering the cafe. I was speechless. It was my brother, Bobby, whom I was going to visit. Afraid that my mind was playing tricks on me, I still called him over. He greeted me with the traditional Alabama Hug. Not saying a word, he sat down. I ordered hamburgers, fries and cokes. I couldn't get him engaged in conversation. All he did was sit there, slowly chewing his food and smiling. There was an eerie look on his face that I had never seen. I was uncomfortable to the point that I couldn't wait to leave. A cold chill seemed to emanate from him. I paid the tab and we headed for the door. Bobby entered the men's room and I waited by the door. After about twenty minutes, I became concerned. He never came out. I checked each stall in the rest room only to find it empty.

My imagination ran wild. I thought perhaps he had deliberately slipped out. I checked with the waitresses and was assured that he had not come back in. I returned to my car to fill the tank before continuing. I pulled up to the pump. The pain returned stronger than ever. I slumped over the steering wheel. As the station attendant revived me, I felt myself leave my body and float upward. My entire being was loose and free from all encumbrances. I felt myself re-enter my body as the pains subsided.

I got back on the road and tuned the radio to an Anniston station about one hundred miles away. The first thing that came over the air rang throughout my entire being. I froze, dripping with cold sweat. The announcer continued, "Heflin youth, Bobby Brown, was pronounced dead early this morning at the scene of a car/truck collision on Route 78 at the foot of Heflin Mountain." Heflin Mountain was another two hundred miles away! When I reached the funeral home hours later, I waited another hour before I could see my brother. After talking with the funeral director, I realized that the sharp pain I had experienced in my heart coincided with the steering column penetrating my brother's chest. The pains in my legs were the pains he experienced as a result of his legs being pinned in the wreckage. This information shed new light on my pain and anguish of the past week.

The following day, a seven-mile-long funeral procession headed from the closely-knit town to a small church outside the city limits. The service was short. Afterward, I found myself standing beside the grave dropping a handful of dirt on the shining white casket.

As I released the dirt, a gentle breeze kissed my cheek and I heard a faint voice saying, "Thanks for lunch. I love you, always remember that." As I returned to my car, I heard the same faint voice calling, "I will see you again."

This was the most difficult story I have ever written. As I sat at the keyboard typing, certain words simply disappeared from the screen. I typed them again. They disappeared again. After changing some words and phrases, they remained as typed. It was as though Bobby had assisted in telling the tale, finally getting his last word in.

It has been over thirty-five years since the tragic accident without any message from Bobby.

On July 9, 2004, my brother Lyle was preparing for a vacation in Florida. Prior to leaving, he purchased a disposable Polaroid camera from a local discount house. I was sitting at my computer when I heard him say, "smile." I was partially turned when he snapped the picture. He pulled it from the camera and headed towards the door. I was pressed by a deadline and ignored the picture. Later that day, I peeled the backing from the picture and saw an amazing clear print of Bobby sitting there by my side infatuated with the mechanics of a computer.

# Heart Patient Watches Own Botched By-Pass

Lyle Brown, an Ohio native, experienced his first heart attack at thirty-seven years of age. Heart diseases were not the norm in his unusually healthy family. Lyle was the first in his family to experience heart problems. He was told at the initial diagnosis that it was merely a situation of pulled muscles surrounding the heart. Eventually, the situation and pain problems became more frequent, resulting in hospitalization. He was rushed immediately into preparation for contiguous surgery.

It was immediately after receiving the anesthetic that Lyle allegedly left his body, rising slowly about four feet above the operating table. He reportedly witnessed the opening of his chest cavity revealing an enlarged heart. "I hovered above my body watching every move of the surgeon's scalpel," he said, somewhat despondent. I questioned the tone in his voice, and he continued, "I saw the scalpel slip and puncture my lung. I also witnessed about half my lung being removed and seared together with silver nitrate. The pain was excruciating. I felt every second of it," he added. Lyle wondered why part of the lung was being removed. Five of his ribs were broken in the pre-operation preparation. During the operation, a sixth rib was broken and removed completely, leaving only a ragged stub.

After he awoke in recovery, Lyle asked for his dentures and glasses that had been removed prior to surgery. The nurse could not locate them and came back with no possible explanation as to what could have happened to them. Lyle told her the teeth and glasses had been placed on a shelf directly behind his head. The nurse explained that he could not possibly know where the items were as he was under the anesthetic. Lyle explained that only moments after receiving the anesthetic, he floated out of his body and hovered only feet above the operating table for the entire operation. He witnessed everything. Moments later, the nurse returned with his teeth and glasses. "I don't understand how you could have known that; I don't understand," she said, "but it is eerie and gives me chills." Lyle added, "I also know about the episode with the lung."

After recovery, Lyle called the surgeon with his allegation that he had slipped and punctured the lung with the scalpel. The surgeon called it absurd and refused further dialog. According to him, only minor scar tissue was removed from the lung; and therefore, the issue was dismissed. It wasn't until two years later, after a car accident, that Lyle had the necessity of getting more x-rays.

The nurse told him that it appeared as though in addition to major quadruple by-pass surgery, he also had almost half a lung removed. Lyle played coy and agreed, asking jokingly to see the x-rays. As a paramedic, he recognized that half his lung had been removed. It was reported that a young girl had been waiting for a lung the same time as Lyle's surgery. It appeared that she had mysteriously received one.

After weeks and months of trying to retrieve the X-rays, medical records, and other pertinent documents, Lyle felt he was ready to present his findings to a medical mal-practice lawyer. His first two interviews were with attorneys who admitted being golf partners with the surgeon and claimed that a conflict of interest prohibited them from taking his case. Other lawyers asked if he had x-rays showing that he actually had two full lungs prior to surgery. After six years of exhaustive effort, Lyle finally admitted defeat.

Lyle's experience reminds me of when I bought four new nail-proof tires for my car. After taking it to a local garage for a tune-up, I got the car back with four completely different tires. When I confronted the mechanic, the garage owner said, "Do you have photographic proof that the four tires you got back were not the same four you had when you came in? If not, bug off and stop harassing me." Thankfully, that garage owner is now out of business. He was eventually caught and prosecuted. The same should happen to unscrupulous doctors.

Perhaps there is justice somewhere, but I no longer think she is blind. Lady Justice can definitely see. After ENRON and the episode with gas prices, I also think she is a crook.

# THE CURSE OF MADISON AVENUE
### And how it made a prediction come true

In the late sixties, I operated a small print shop on Mulberry Street in North Toledo, Ohio. I attended the Spiritualist Church on Western Avenue. It was a ritual every Sunday for me to schedule the mid-morning sermon. I was editor of a monthly publication, THE PSYCHIC EYE and was always looking for new material. The church usually proved to be a never-ending source. One Sunday proved to be extremely interesting, but I did not know it would take over a decade to act itself out. I had never received a reading at the church. I attributed that to the fact that I never discussed my personal life with anyone there. A gathering in the dining hall always drew a large crowd prior to the sermon. Everyone was anxious to get a reading. A few ministers and psychics were always in attendance and willing to exhibit their talents. They always engaged in conversation prior to the readings.

In casual conversation, one would disclose his ancestry, deceased relatives, business affairs and other idle chitchat. I noticed those "talkers" were always the ones who received messages from the minister or psychic at the podium. In ten years, I had never received a message other than a "tube sock" message, "one size fits all."

This particular Sunday, I was the first person the message bearer selected. A reader who was visiting from

Detroit told me I was planning a business move. She said it would be "near Madison Avenue, but not on Madison. Stay away from Madison Avenue. You will try and try again, but Madison is not in your future. That street can only bring you grief."

At the time, I had made no such plans. When I returned home, a friend was waiting on the porch. Jim O'Brien, a long time friend and fellow printer, had decided to move to Florida where his aging mother would reap the benefits of milder winters. Toledo winters were terrible, and he too was beginning to feel the pains of harsh weather. Jim had just purchased a new sixty-foot trailer and offered to sell it to me. Since I had just purchased my home, I was not interested. We had coffee, and he told me of his plans to sell his print shop, which he had recently relocated to Tenth Street, at Madison. I did not associate the address at the time, and the conversation continued.

About two hours later, Jim had to leave to assist his mother with her injections. He turned to me at the last minute and said, "Why don't you buy my print shop?" He offered me his entire printing and rubber stamp shop for a mere cash payment of $5,000. Without hesitation, I gave him a deposit of $1,000 and promised the balance the following day. Within a week, my assistant, Colleen Wooten, our pressman, and I began the tedious task of moving an entire print shop. The next few weeks kept us busy, and I had not returned to church because Sundays demanded I sleep most of the day to catch up on my rest.

A month later, we had the signs painted on the two eight-foot windows and were open for business. I ran ads in the newspaper and purchased radio advertising announcing our grand opening. Opening day turned out to be a total disaster. The only activity in the shop was neighbors stopping in to give us their blessings.

The following week, I was back at church. I was late, but as I entered the chapel, I remembered "Madison Avenue." Again, that Sunday, I left without a reading. As always, I had not talked about my family or problems to anyone in the dining area.

This Sunday proved interesting, as there were many visitors from out of state. They all received remarkable readings giving names, dates and places. I was amazed as each visitor confessed they knew no one there and had never visited the church.

The next morning, at 2:30 a.m., the Toledo Police called me. My building was on fire. I reached the shop in less than ten minutes, and the alarm was still sounding. The windows were knocked out, the ceiling and apartment furniture upstairs had fallen into my shop and the water damage was enormous. I was out of business!

I notified my insurance company later that day, and appraisers were sent in from Cleveland to assess the damage. Since I had recently acquired the shop and the inventory, I did not have adequate insurance to cover it. My policy, which transferred from the other shop, did not even cover one-fourth of the damage. I was devastated.

The office manager at Mid Am Bank gave me an advance on the insurance settlement, and I immediately began looking for another building. I found one with the assistance of an old friend. I leased the front of the Waldorf

Hotel, a Toledo Landmark at Summit and Madison. The next few weeks, we were busy acquiring new equipment and supplies to re-open

I spent about half the insurance settlement in remodeling the shop area and wasted no time in re-opening. I not only had my livelihood to worry about, but that of my employees, as well.

The new shop on Summit Street, at Madison, in the heart of Toledo, started off well. We were across from the Toledo Federal Building, Toledo Trust Bank and Toledo Edison. All were high-rise office buildings and gave us an immediate boost in revenue. It was about two months before our new camera arrived from Chicago. As we were installing our camera, the hotel manager came in with an eviction notice. The building was being torn down for a new Toledo Trust building. Residents and tenants with six months tenancy received relocation pay. We received sympathetic comments.

When the month's rent was up, I loaded a rental truck and headed back to my own building on Mulberry Street. When I arrived back home, I felt a sinking feeling. I knew it would never be the same as before.

After I re-opened, neighbors began complaining about UPS and large paper trucks stopping everyday and blocking the alley. My building was on the dividing line between residential and commercial properties. Heretofore, there had been no problems because of my years at that location. However, upon my return, everyone seemed to have some type of complaint.

The next Sunday, I went back to church; and this time I invited my brother, Lyle, to go with me. He was always skeptical and didn't really expect much. About halfway through the sermon, a man on the other side of the chapel came over and handed Lyle a note. The contents of the note were not made known to me until days later. Lyle took it as a joke and discarded it. A few days later, he told me the note foretold a move for him. Lyle had not been planning any move and thought no more about it. The following day, he stopped in after work and told me he had quit his job and was moving to Arizona. Lyle laughingly said, "The old man was right about a move, but wrong about the direction. He said I would not move west, but south. Unless Arizona has moved, I am heading west tomorrow."

I didn't get much sleep that night, thinking about my only Ohio family member leaving Toledo. Floyd, my other brother, lived in South Carolina. When Lyle came over to say goodbye, I told him I was moving too. At the last moment, I had decided to move to Florida. I invited Lyle to travel with me to Florida and promised that after unloading my equipment, I would go to Arizona with him for a few days.

We rented a truck and trailer, and two days later were off to Florida. We arrived in Daytona Beach and began the tedious search for an appropriate building. We found one the next day and began unloading. Daytona Beach had certain license requirements that I had never heard of in Toledo. By the time I paid for all the licenses, high utility deposits, insurance, a sign, a six-month lease deposit, supplies, and looked for an apartment, I was broke. Lyle stayed with me in Florida for a couple of weeks and paid for the boarding house we shared. I bought a $2,500 advertising package announcing my grand opening. As luck would have it, Hurricane David hit Daytona. The area was evacuated, and I did not have one customer. The police drove up and down the streets announcing evacuation. Lyle and I stayed in the back of the shop with the lights off and refused to leave.

Two months later, Lyle was still in Florida helping me run the shop. I knew he would never make it to Arizona. That part of the prediction had come true. Little did I know at the time, my own prediction was just beginning. We returned to Toledo to get the rest of our equipment from storage. It was Sunday, so we decided to go to Church in hopes of receiving some encouragement.

The same reader from Detroit was visiting Toledo again, and she immediately came to me. She said in an authoritative manner, "You made a mistake when you moved. You were not supposed to move out of Toledo. I see a black iron fence going around a hundred-year-old church. I see a white iron fence of the same kind, across the street around a modem building." I had no idea what she meant. I could not believe the move to Florida could in anyway hurt my already gravely distressed business. I was frustrated and could not associate with anything she said. After the sermon and message session, everyone went to the dining hall for coffee. Since we were leaving for Florida, we decided to have a cup before the trip. While enjoying a hot cup of coffee, the minister came over to our table and gave me a note. The note said, "Ohio is your home. Look for the old building. I think it is a church. It is a mistake to leave Ohio."

We finished our coffee and headed back to Florida. The normal forty-eight hour trip, driving a truck, was made in thirty-six hours. I couldn't get the psychic's message out of my mind. When we returned to Florida, we were greeted by the landlord. He informed us that the building was up for sale and our lease would not be renewed. Our landlord, a religious and understanding gentleman, gave his permission to break the lease in order to seek other accommodations.

The move to Florida had exhausted all my funds and Lyle's savings as well. I already owed him thousands of dollars that he had spent on my behalf moving to Florida. We began searching that day for a new location. We found one about two miles from our current location. I met with the owner, and he offered me immediate occupancy with no deposit. I thought my luck was finally changing. After leaving, I realized I had rented a building on *Madison Avenue*. We returned the following day with our first load of equipment, only to find a note on the door. The note reported the death of the owner and plans for his son to open the location as a flower shop.

I called a friend and noted psychic in Cleveland, Ohio, Molly Swingler. Molly invited me to move to Cleveland and offered her vast knowledge of the city to help us relocate. We accepted the invitation and arrived in Cleveland four days later. Once again, we began the tedious search for a building. We located a building on *Madison Avenue,* just outside Cleveland. The rent was nine hundred dollars a month, far more than I had ever paid for any previous building. At this point, I was desperate and Molly offered to loan me the money. The little village was unique with matching awnings, signs, and decor throughout the area. The owner of the Madison Avenue building had told us that since we are a medium commercial manufacturing company, the lease would have to be approved by city council. We were to come back in two days.

I later told Molly about my message from the Spiritualist Minister about "Madison Avenue" and the "two iron fences". We looked up and down the street but could not find such a fence, or any building that was a hundred years old. We went to lunch and then back to Molly's apartment. The following day, we returned to our new Madison Avenue address. The rental agent looked uneasy as we approached him. I knew the Madison Avenue curse had struck again. The type of equipment used in our shop exceeded the noise regulations, and the fumes produced from our rubber stamp equipment were prohibited.

Lyle and I took Molly back home, and headed for Toledo. We stopped at a motel across from the YMCA in Toledo. We pulled our truck and trailer around to the side and took accommodations for the night. We were now completely broke and living on credit cards. Time was critical, and we had to make every minute productive. We began looking at real estate books, walking the streets and making inquiries whenever possible about the availability of, at this point, *any* vacant building.

The next morning, we were up at daylight going through the paces again. We located a building at 1010 *Madison Avenue*, across the street from my former shop on Tenth Street. I knew it was Madison Avenue, but I was desperate! I contacted the owner and made arrangements to move in the next day; we had no utilities, no apartment, nothing! Both Lyle and I were excited, though we wondered how we could pay the high rent plus an apartment. "Things will work out," I told him.

Lyle was a younger brother, and I always felt responsible for him. We returned to the Lorraine Hotel, just two blocks from our new shop, only to find where our truck and trailer had been parked, all that remained was a pile of broken glass. The truck, trailer, and all the contents had been stolen. We notified the Toledo Police Department and filed a report by phone. No police officer ever showed up. I immediately notified the local TV stations, and they were there within minutes.

After the commotion was over, I called Molly in Cleveland and told her what had happened. Molly, who had been my personal psychic for years, immediately began seeing images. She said, "Your equipment is across the river. I see a ravine and a dirt road. Most of your equipment will never be recovered, but you will recover enough to get back into business." That was the only consolation. I was desperate. I called another psychic, Patricia A. Huff, Director of the MESA Parapsychology Center in Toledo. Since I didn't have any transportation, Pat agreed to come to me. She soon arrived with her assistant, Bob Jacobs. I told Pat and Bob what Molly had seen in her visions. We crossed the river to the east side and wound up on "Ravine Park." We drove around for hours looking for a dirt road. We found it, Berlin Street. It was a short dirt road with only a few houses.

We drove up and down, stopped and looked, and found nothing. All the houses looked occupied. Obviously, no one would park a stolen truck and trailer there. The search continued on into the night. We ended at Frisches Big Boy for supper, and later called it a night. Pat and Bob delivered us back to our hotel.

The next day, I received a call from the desk clerk. The police had located my equipment. I phoned the police and discovered that the trailer was behind the exact house where our psychic detective group had stopped in front of twice, the night before. We had turned around in the driveway, but had we gone just another two feet, we would have seen our trailer. It was exactly where the Cleveland psychic said it would be. The house looked lived in, but the tenants had abandoned it. The curtains were still hanging, but there was little furniture. Pieces of printing equipment were scattered about the house and back yard. Some of the smaller pieces had been buried, possibly for later retrieval. Instead of giving me the opportunity to move it, the Toledo Police called a private mover to pick up everything and take it to his storage building. This incurred another unexpected out-of-pocket expense. At this point, we began taking loans out on the few credit cards available. We both knew that soon our credit would be cancelled.

Days later, we retrieved our truck with a burned out clutch. It was abandoned and required extensive repair: wiring, clutch and a large dented fender. Lyle repaired the clutch, and I repaired the ignition. We no longer needed a key to start the car; we merely touch the wires together.

We located the storage warehouse and went about getting our equipment back. The owner insisted that some of our supplies and tools belonged to him. After an argument ensued, he threw us out of the building. We hooked up to the trailer with what little was left and hauled it back to the hotel. By this time, everyone knew there was nothing of value in the trailer, so we needed no lock. The desk clerk switched our rooms to where we could keep an eye on the truck at night.

Determined not to let our luck get us down, the next morning found us pounding the pavement looking for another building. Since we lost our equipment, someone else had rented the building on Madison Avenue. It was just as well. I don't think at this point, my sanity could have withstood any move to, or near Madison Avenue.

We began walking to the outskirts of the city, thinking the rent would be cheaper. We walked down Cherry Street to Central Avenue. We came upon the American Legion and went in for a beer. It was hot, and we were exhausted. The Second Vice Commander came over and introduced himself. We explained our dilemma. "I can help you," he smiled. He called the local funeral director and arranged a meeting. The three of us walked to the funeral home, where the funeral director gave us the keys to a nearby building. We couldn't afford to be choosy, so we thanked him and the legionnaire and went in search of the building.

After we exited the funeral home, Lyle noticed a white iron fence. Then he pointed out a black iron fence across the street. We stopped in awe. The white iron fence was around a modern funeral home. The black iron fence across the street was around a hundred-year-old cathedral. We found the building near the funeral home. It needed extensive repairs, but we took that in stride. We figured a few gallons of paint would cover a multitude of sins.

In less than a week, we moved what little equipment and supplies we had into our new building. We had no motor for the press, so the first orders were run completely by hand. We notified our former customers that we were back in Toledo. We offered 1,000 business cards for $4.99 printed one at a time, by hand.

The curse of Madison Avenue had ended. The psychic was right; and although I write about psychic experiences, I am still a skeptic. I now realize that there are real psychics, however hampered they might be by an occasional charlatan.

Our trek from Toledo to Florida, to Cleveland and back to Toledo encompassed over three thousand miles. In actuality, we only moved two streets from Mulberry Street to LaGrange, less than four blocks away. We occupied that building for nearly forty years.

Finally, the computer revolution killed the printing business. It was a great life. The print shop is now closed, and all I have to do to remind me of those fond memories, and unfortunate mishaps, is to sit quietly and commit my thoughts to paper.

I have since moved back to Florida where I collect my thoughts among the tall Laurel Oak trees in a quiet little retirement village in DeLand, Florida.

# PHYSICIAN...
# HEAL THYSELF

I first became interested in healing at the early age of thirteen. It was sad to sit in the chapel and watch the ministers grab ailing members and practically shake their heads off while shouting unknown tongues, often "causing" rather than curing ailments.

I often left the church with tears in my eyes for the older women who went forward for relief. Some of them returned to their seats somewhat comforted, while others continued to house agonizing pain.

Years later, I learned of the various brain patterns, frequencies and releasing techniques necessary to acquire the desired result.

I began visiting the various churches: Baptist, Methodist, Mormon and others, comparing healing techniques. I always felt that everyone could be a healer because the bible says, "Physician, heal thyself." One only has to recognize that he is but a channel for healing through the universal consciousness. This consciousness is linked to the soul of all mankind. Look for this union and recognize the power within yourself and accept and transmit the energy, which is readily available to you. I have respect for any sincere healer, regardless of the methods he employs. As a church member has faith in God, or a higher being, he also places his trust in the minister who teaches him. If either factor were absent, one less seat would fill the pews.

Man uses less than ten percent of his brain capacity. As most ailments are "self inflicted," why can "self" not cure those same illnesses? The need for sickness is often the inner consciousness carrying out a subliminal plan for the end result of a preconceived act. If you are scheduled to give a lecture and are unprepared, why not develop a sore throat or headache? How many children get sick in school and are perfectly normal upon arriving back at home? The complex organ we call the mind does not know if we are actually sick. Have you ever been on a date and said you had a headache, to find moments later that you "actually" had one, subconsciously sending thoughts to the brain that we are physically ill? The majority of ailments disappear as soon as the cause is dissolved. Have you ever developed a headache when you had company, only to find it completely gone as soon as your guests leave?

It's called *"programming."* You are actually sending (conscious or unconscious) messages to the brain, which produce positive or negative results. Next time you tell someone that you have an ailment, remember, *"Thoughts are things."* In the same respect that a thought is a thing, also remember that thoughts have wings. In many cases, the same thoughts that cause an ailment, while transmitting to the brain, often transfer to the brain of someone else. Not always is the message interpreted or recognized, but it's there. How many times has someone given you a most serious excuse not to do something? You knew they were lying through their teeth. Take a few minutes to think about this.

Numerous healing techniques exist. Regardless of the method employed, have your own body and mind in harmony before taking the first step. Jesus, a great psychic and healer, was always in tune with the universal mind consciousness or God consciousness. Set your thoughts in order. Take a few moments in a secluded place and tell yourself what you earnestly believe about life and the Godhead. Many religious leaders will tell you that hell is a burning fire; others say it is in your heart. Still others are convinced that we are serving hell on earth, and death is heaven, true bliss.

Empty your mind of all garbage, all negative thoughts and ill will against everyone. You may have convictions that you don't want to admit. Acknowledge them. Healings, whether done on someone else, or on you, are not done for praise or money. Consider it to be a star in your crown, a crown that only you and God see. Remember, "Like attracts like." You are the architect of your own constellation, one of which the majority is your own inner being.

Many healers believe in the Bible and a supreme being. Others don't recognize God and consider the Bible nothing more than a book written by people trying to instill fear in the hearts of the evildoers. Margie Woods, a healer from Pennsylvania, reads the Bible before performing any type of healing. She has someone hold the Bible over the recipient's head while she anoints the patient with coconut oil, a special blend from the Philippines. This is a perfect example of a healer who believes in her work. All donations from lectures and healings go to the Philippines to build a much-needed medical center. She keeps not one cent for herself

For every healer that prepares for healings, through meditation, chants, reading the Bible, ritualistic bathing, or fasting, there are those that don't consider preparation necessary.

Healers like Dr. Ralph U. Sierra, of Puerto Rico, employs a uniquely different technique in healings. Biomagnetism is the art of healing through the power of magnets and concentration. It is difficult to determine exactly how much of the healing is performed strictly through the use of magnets as compared to the percent of healings through the power of the mind. The technique is highly effective. He built a large pyramid near his laboratory and had remarkable success through pyramid power.

Zone therapy is a very relaxing method of healing. This is a process of simple massage. Such therapy is the applying of pressure to specific points on the hands, feet and other parts of the body to relieve pain. There are many books available on this subject and it would be worth one's time to study these techniques as they can be performed in their purest simplicity. When one becomes ill, the force that gives life to cells crystallizes at various points in the body coinciding with the afflicted areas. This crystallization occurs at the acupuncture points of the body or points of entry of the vital force. Zone therapy techniques dislodge these crystals, clearing the passageways. When the corresponding foot organ is infected, the foot will develop a tender or hardened area. Gentle massage of that area will break the crystals and allow the force to flow. As the crystals dissolve, the symptoms dissipate. This is particularly effective in certain cases of arthritis, thus allowing healing. Therapy is most practical when practiced just before bed. Five to ten minutes daily will be a tremendous aid to better health. By employing this technique on a regular basis, you can detect a sensitive spot and possibly prevent an ailment. In addition to a healthier lifestyle, you will be more energized. A coke bottle rolled back and forth on the floor while applying pressure with your feet is not only relaxing, but also beneficial in alleviating stress and preventing many problems.

Laying on of hands is a technique that has been used since the days of Jesus in Jerusalem. However, this is not recommended unless you are a licensed minister. Laws in different states frown on this practice. One must be cautioned that with any healing technique, unless you are a doctor or licensed minister, you might be asking for problems.

It is always wise to be careful when doing healings on anyone. Never touch anyone below the shoulders. It is usually okay to touch the hands, head or shoulders. Anything other than those points is usually taboo. There are simply too many people waiting for an opportunity for a lawsuit.

# ANCIENT LADY SAVES NEWSPAPER OFFICE

The Lady of Crete is allegedly a native to the Island of Crete. She is fashioned of molten lava and her life span has already exceeded two hundred years. This ancient museum piece has been passed from one person to another in the Toledo area for over one hundred years.

Legend has it that the Lady, devoid of eyes, is an ancient protector and guardian of the dead. She has no eyes as she gazes upon the soul and not the body. In addition to guarding and directing the departed souls to a higher level, she acts as a centurion protector of her owner. While disaster will allegedly befall anyone who steals her or comes by her through monetary gain, she can be passed on lovingly from one person to another. If her current owner dies, she must remain in the house and become the protector of the closest relative residing at the same address.

The penetrating emptiness of her eyes sees into the soul of all who come within her gaze. In the event of imminent danger to her guardian, she turns a deadly shade of gray. In 1971, she graced the office of the *Psychic Eye Newspaper*, (now, *Body, Mind & Spirit News*) in downtown Toledo where she stood vigil for years. Her complacency remained steady. Colleen, the assistant manager, noticed one day that her earthen brown color was starting to fade. Three days later, she was slate gray. This caused considerable concern for the owner. After a frustrating day of breakdowns, the office closed with no other unusual activity.

The next morning at three o'clock, a call from the Toledo Fire Department awakened the entire Brown household. The downtown publishing office was engulfed in flames. The entire shop was destroyed. The office containing the Lady remained intact and suffered no damage. With two pumpers on the scene, pouring thousands of gallons of water on the flames, the office where the Lady resided, sustained no water or smoke damage. Hundreds of antique and out of print books remained in pristine condition and suffered no smoke damage.

The Lady now resides in the *Body, Mind & Spirit Newspaper* office in Toledo, Ohio. On May 11, 2004, Molly Swingler, a noted Cleveland psychic, was visiting the Brown brothers, editor and publishers of the newspaper. Molly, who was also present at a fire that claimed a death in downtown Toledo, was very much aware of the unique legend of the Lady of Crete. She commented, that she did not remember the Lady being so gray. "I always remembered her as being browner," she added. Charlie, the editor of the paper observed the Lady as deathly gray. She was sitting on a computer desk in the west side of the building. The shade of gray was simply attributed to the sun and it was dismissed. During a power failure that evening, everyone sat on the patio to await repairs. The doors to the building were closed and nothing seemed unusual. About an hour later, the door mysteriously came open and a glow was noticed inside. Lyle mentioned the glow, but it was thought to be candles. "That's no candle," he exclaimed. "That looks like a fire." He ran into the building to find the office filled with a heavy black smoke. The entertainment center housing the television and other electronics was all slightly visible through the black pitch smoke. He grabbed the phone and ran outside calling for help. The phone was dead, and there was no recourse but to try to save the building. All three people grabbed fire extinguishers, and in seconds extinguished the flames. The electronics including the newspaper laptop computer, answering machine, telephone, and entertainment center cabinet were destroyed. The office remained no less for damage, other than needing a new paint job, drapes and incidentals.

Once again, the ever vigil Lady of Crete saved the day. Thanks to the legend of the unfaltering dedication to her owner, the Newspaper office has surpassed another possibly devastating hurdle. Each adjacent room to the office sustained major smoke damage. The office where the Lady sat was left without either smoke damage or the noxious odor of burning plastic.

# PSYCHICS OF SUBSTANCE

My first experience worth mention was in 1952 with my doting grandmother telling me how to remove a large wart from my knee. I was crazy about baseball, and every game would end with the same bloody knee when the wart got torn off. A few weeks afterward, it would grow back even larger than before. Finally, my grandmother placed a wet towel on my knee, said a prayer and ordered me to hold the cloth tightly for three minutes. At the end of this ritual, I was instructed to bury the towel on the bank of a nearby stream where the water would cover the burial site. Within seven days, the wart fell off never to return. As the water washed the dirt from the burial site down the stream, the wart was also washed permanently from my knee. After more than fifty years, the wart has never returned.

In 1999, my brother was scheduled to have extrinsic spinal spurs surgically removed from his throat. They had grown to a proportion that hampered simple tasks like breathing and eating. Lady Maleva from Cleveland, Ohio, a well-known spiritual healer and psychic, was in Toledo for a holiday. She did a simple "laying on of the hands" and recited a simple prayer. She gently massaged the swollen area as she concentrated on the calcium deposits dissolving. Lyle had also already been diagnosed with spinal spurs, and their presence were apparent as a result of a battery of X-rays. A doctor at St. Vincent Hospital in Toledo had scheduled surgery in two weeks. During this period, Lyle had two other healing sessions by the Cleveland psychic. The scheduled day of surgery, he was admitted early in the morning.

Prior to the operation, the doctor ordered another set of x-rays to see if any change had occurred. "This is not funny," he shouted at the x-ray technician. "You brought me the wrong x-rays!" A second set of x-rays was taken and still no sign of spinal spurs were present. The doctor could not explain the disappearance of the calcium spurs. "They just don't disappear," he said. "These did!" Lyle answered, and he was discharged without surgery.

In the late 1970's, my brother, Floyd had his foot crushed at a Toledo Steel plant. He was admitted to Riverside Hospital. He called me and told me of the possibility of having to remove his foot due to the massive fractures. At the time, MESA (Metaphysical, Esoteric, Sciences Association) under the direction of the late Pat Huff had their office in the Heflin Building on Mulberry Street in North Toledo. Pat summoned her group to do an "absent" healing on Floyd. The sitting lasted about an hour. This was done prior to my visit to the hospital. When I arrived at the hospital, Floyd was sitting up in good spirits. He told me the first set of x-rays had been bad, but a new set of x-rays revealed no fractures. He was dismissed the next day. The x-ray technician swore the first set of pictures were accurate but was at a loss as to the miraculous change.

In June 2004, I received a reading from Sharon Kay of Trinity Spiritualist Church in Toledo, Ohio. She was a student of Pat Huff and performed her ritualistic reading in the same fashion as Pat. It was a rather lengthy ritual, but

Sharon, which seemed to work rather well, had adopted a somewhat shortened version. Sharon started out with an Irish accent, which was at times difficult to understand. Her voice changed occasionally as if assisted by another entity. Sharon told me that I would soon do a healing on someone's knee. I had absolutely no idea as to what she meant. She suggested the healing might possibly be at a hospital. The last time I visited a hospital had been about a year prior, when I visited a friend in the burn unit at St. Vincent's hospital. I didn't anticipate a visit to any hospital anytime soon.

Three days later, my brother Lyle walked out of our office door during a ninety-degree and higher heat wave. The heat caused him to become unstable, and he fell off the top step onto the sidewalk. Since he was a heart patient, I immediately grabbed the phone to call for an ambulance. By this time, neighbors offering their assistance surrounded him. He regained consciousness and said nothing was broken. His knee was severely cut as was his arm, and shoulder. He ordered the ambulance cancelled, shouting, and "No hospital No hospital!" Five minutes later, I was performing first aid on the knee that Sharon had predicted only three days before.

Mac McGuinn, a very dear friend and devoted spiritualist minister, told me time and time again to beware of "tube-sock readings" where one sock fits all. During my lifetime, I have had experiences with many such readers. I have had some good and some...well...! While on vacation, my car broke down in a small southern town. There was a flea market across from the mechanic's garage. A reader had her gaudy sign displayed in such a fashion that even the blind could see it, "*Readings* $5." I didn't expect much for five dollars. She began by asking me questions in an extremely poor attempt to gain information. I volunteered nothing. She continued her spiel on death, doom and destruction. She told me I had a bad spell on me. "For two hundred fifty dollars, I will remove it," she said. "Someone is trying to take your money and do you harm." When I told her how much it would cost to repair my car, she offered to break the spell for fifty dollars, providing I go to a nearby store and buy fifty dollars worth of candles and incense. This would save her valuable time that she could devote to breaking the spell. I told the old lady that I was "not afraid of any spell. I invoke the law of three, 'what goes around, comes around." She became angry and asked me to leave.

On August 2, 2003, at Psychic Sunday, a program sponsored by the *Psychic Eye Newspaper* at the First Spiritualist Church in Toledo, I was asked to be moderator. I accepted, and as my first act, I appointed Betty Moses to be moderator. I sat back and relaxed. I was recovering from cancer and had lost about seventy pounds. During the awards ceremony, I lost a valuable diamond ring. After retracing my footsteps, I could not find the ring. Fortunately there were many psychics present who I held in high esteem. I asked Linda Dix if she could locate the ring for me. After a few seconds, she told me it was in the garbage. During my awards presentation, I had placed a waste paper basket by the microphone to dispose of the wrappings from the awards. While disposing of paper, the ring slipped off and fell into the garbage can. Linda told me she saw the ring embedded in newspaper and litter, and that was exactly where I located it.

In May of 2004, Molly Swingler was visiting from Cleveland, Ohio. I had been writing articles for magazines and newspapers for over forty years. I had published three books. After all the pounding of keys, I had never been paid for any of the articles. I asked Molly if I would ever get paid for any of my work. Her prompt reply was, "Yes, you are going to get published in *FATE®* magazine, maybe more than once. In the middle of July, I was surprised by a call from Linda Dix informing me that she had seen one of my stories in *FATE®*. In less than a year, I received another call from Linda. A second story appeared in *FATE®*. My stories still appear in FATE® on a regular basis.

In all the years of publishing, I am constantly asked the same question, "Are psychics real?" I hope this brief synopsis has shed some light on the subject. Although there are many charlatans out there who are simply after the almighty dollar, there are still some honest, dedicated psychics around. One has but to look first and ask questions second. Never volunteer any information. You don't want to pay to have your voluntary information turned around and given back to you. Although most psychics charge a fee, there are still those who do it strictly for the joy of helping others. I have found those precious few to be more accurate.

# RETURN TO OUR ROOTS

We are often reminded of our younger years when we didn't know if we would have food on the table. Today we view those days as a by-gone era. We don't think of where our next meal will come from. We don't ponder on where we will sleep for the night. We can't even imagine not having a warm blanket to snuggle up in on those long, cold, blustery winter nights. Though many of us migrated to the north like the annual bird flow, we still realize that it can get cold no matter where we are.

The spirit of those former days was wrapped in the warmth of a common bond between family and friends. We were never alone. We had continued support from each member of our family to give us the strength to continue our daily struggle for survival. The love and peace of mind and warmth that we received from being a whole family instead of a single person wrapped us in the comfort and knowledge that we would survive. *"Where there is a will, there is a way."* Many of us remember that slogan and recite it as part of our silent daily prayers. It was something that was embedded in our psyche. Somehow, we knew through our inner being, our guardian angel, our protector, our guide, or perhaps the simple peace of knowing, that we had a God that brought us through each day.

It is that same kinship that we must rekindle within ourselves, and our family and friends, that is necessary to keep us sane, as these latter days bring more and more hardship. We must rekindle that spark as more and more of our friends and associates become unemployed, file bankruptcy, lose their homes, stand in food lines and fight to maintain their sanity.

The uphill road that we are traversing at this point in time will eventually start to reach a curve where the road gradually starts an incline. The incline will reach a hill, and the hill will soon turn into a mountain.

The budget for many social services has been cut to the bone, and those funds are being redirected to a war in Iraq. The cuts in Medicaid have already jolted millions of people when they went to the drug store to find out that some of the medication they have been taking for years is no longer covered. Our senior citizens are already struggling; these compounding problems with their health bring more fright to their already mind-altering dilemma. If we think we had problems in our formative years, just wait.

Those who were secure in their union jobs are now facing layoffs, pay freezes, and uncertainty. The Legal Aid Society is reporting that each of their representatives is faced with a backlog of fifteen hundred cases, most being of bankruptcy. The number is rapidly reaching ten thousand cases in our area, and I predict it will go much, much higher.

The situation with oil and gas prices going up and down is a total joke! This situation has been brought upon us by the greed of the Americans who sold our oil reserves to overseas conglomerates. The Alaskan Pipeline that was supposed to be our salvation is now the property of overseas owners. We were told that sending manufacturing to Mexico would help the economy. Southern furniture jobs are being sent overseas. More and more people are hitting the bread line on a daily basis. Yet, we are told the economy is on an upward trend with unemployment holding at 6.25 percent last month. Are we supposed to be impressed, or do we still face financial ruin?

This is the time for family bonding. This is the time for the family to bring peace back into the home. This is the time for meditation, understanding, solace, and prayer. This is the time for us to realize and bring into focus that our nation is founded on "In God we trust." It seems that certain aristocrats think nothing more than tearing down that infrastructure. Dump the Ten Commandments. Help to foster and perpetuate a plan to destroy the nation already in its worst struggle in present memory. We don't have enough problems in our nation, in our government. Let's see what dirt we can unearth and cause a few more problems; incite a little more unrest.

Another perfect example can be seen any day on our interstate highways, city and county roads. We have even forgotten how to drive. Road rage seems to be the norm. We already have enough stress without adding to the already steadily increasing problems.

After thinking about it, I have come to the conclusion that our roots weren't so bad after all!

# THE ART OF WISHFUL THINKING

It is often said, "Anything you can imagine, you can achieve; and anything that you can visualize, you can become." If this is the case, why is the world in such a turbulent state of devastation? Our faith is somewhat diminished in these latter days. We read the paper only to see blood red between each line of petroleum base black ink. We turn on the radio and hear only devastation. The television networks thrive on tragedies, chaos and unthinkable acts. They won't report the Nobel Peace Prize when they can break in with a disaster situation even though it is a world away.

Racism, riots, muggings, and even the copious amounts of litter we see downgrading our communities, cities and country is constantly bombarding our brain, our mind, and our total being to the point that it is no wonder we cannot form a positive image in our mind.

We look out our window even in the business districts and witness all manner of negative acts. When was the last time you saw someone help an old lady cross the street or a gentleman tip his hat to one, or even walk an extra five feet to dispose of a candy wrapper or cigarette pack? Why not drop it on the sidewalk or throw it out the car window. Better yet, why not take the entire daily trash home and scatter it on our living room floor! At least that way, we are walking in our own filth and not being subjected to the trash of unknown passers-by.

Each of these acts has a negative impact and a continuous bombardment on our psyche. Each negative act we witness requires hours of peace and reflection to overcome each negative thought.

Meditation is becoming more and more a thing of the past in this hectic world; jobs that we hate, children, daily activities, annoying neighbor's boom boxes and the constant bombardment of foul language that we have grown to know and accept as part of our daily routine.

Not many of us can retreat to a secluded tropical island where we can commune with nature and return to the basics. We can, however, return to the ritualistic practices that we know to benefit us, physically, emotionally and spiritually.

The sacrifice of only a half hour a day of solace, stolen from our inordinately busy schedule can assist in the hectic and rocky road to recovery of our sanity, something that we are all going to need in these turbulent days ahead.

A perfect example was my desire to obtain a color 11x17" laser copier. I found one at an auction for only fifteen hundred dollars. After two issues of color, the machine broke down. Toledo had no technician to service this machine. I called Detroit, Cleveland and Chicago. We finally located the same repairman who had previously serviced the machine. He gave me an approximate repair tag of forty-eight hundred dollars. This would give me a completely rebuilt machine that should last for years. After the repairs, we needed a full cache of toner, fuser oil, etc. That cost another fifteen hundred dollars. Nothing else could go wrong. We were then set up for color for the next five years.

The next issue took its toll on our press and it bit the dust. The cost of replacement would be approximately twenty thousand dollars. At that point, we transformed our monthly magazine to tabloid format, not lending itself to color photographs. We had a rebuilt copier with absolutely no use for it. We advertised it for sale for months. Due to the size and complexity of the machine, no one wanted it. One of our employees offered to take it off our hands for two hundred fifty dollars. He had plans of starting a "New Age" paper focusing on healings, meditation, herbs, astrology, etc. We sold it to a competitor for pennies.

That experience caused me to re-evaluate the phrase, *"Be careful what you wish for, you may get it!"* It's more than a wish! The thought that goes into such a program should be clear and precise. The thought energies I sent out never took into consideration that what I really wanted and needed, was a machine in good condition. I really did not want one that was going to cost and "waste" thousands of dollars. This article is not meant to cry over spilled milk, but to make a point. Sometimes we don't "really" want what we think.

In 1998 there was a man in Tennessee who kept praying for a new heart. He knew he only had a few months to live without a transplant. He was retired without a lot of financial resources and insurance. He knew his chances of receiving a heart was not on the top of the list of those who could buy and sell the state of Tennessee.

On his deathbed, he asked to have his children by his side. His son and daughter-in-law flew in from California. After renting a car at the airport, they headed for the small town over a hundred miles away. The weather was bad and the roads were caked with three inches of ice. The car spun out of control and hit a bridge. The son later died in the hospital as a result of his injuries. His wife and children escaped with minor bruises.

The old man lost a son in this tragedy, but gained a new heart. Is it worth getting what we wish for? Sometimes, I think not! Be careful of what YOU wish for. You may not really want it after all.

# TWO SECONDS FROM ETERNITY

Sparky, a loyal reader and supporter of *bodymindspiritnews.com* recalls countless incidents that he refers to as "two seconds from eternity." He recounts an incident in 1958 when he, two classmates and a brother went rafting in the Rogue River in Dearborn, Michigan.

Sparky's foot got caught in roots on the riverbed and he could not surface. His brother and two classmates were too far out to help. He felt a hand grasp the back of his shirt and gently pull him out of the water and place him on the bank. The three others witnessed the incident but were so frightened they vowed never to speak of it. After four decades, Sparky decided to break the silence.

Fire destroyed Sparky's home when he was six. He vividly remembers an angel guiding him to the location of each of the five siblings and helping drag them to safety. "It was like I was being pulled by the hand," he recalls. He was led through blinding, choking smoke to safely evacuate each brother and sister.

Sparky's mother was downstairs watching a late TV show when the fire broke out. She was separated from the sleeping children by an impenetrable wall of fire. A neighbor rushed in and pulled the frantic woman from the inferno. Unaware of the safe evacuation of her children, she suffered a stroke resulting in hospitalization. The possibility of her children perishing in the flames caused recovery to become extremely slow and difficult. During the five years of his mother's therapy, the children were taken to the Goodwill Farm Children's home in Houghton, Michigan.

Each day, the angel returned to visit Sparky. No one could see the angel, including his brothers and sisters. Sparky told them the angel was helping to keep the family together.

During the second year at the orphanage, Sparky's youngest sister was adopted. "What about your angel now?" his brothers jeered. "The angel will bring us back together," Sparky told them.

The next three years brought the children closer together. After years of repetition, Sparky finally convinced them that the angel would bring the whole family back together. The next day, Sparky's mother and uncle arrived at the orphanage. She had come to retrieve her children. Sparky told his mother that the youngest daughter had been adopted. "Don't worry," he assured her. "My angel told me that we would all be back together."

In the 1960's, it was difficult to regain a child after it had been adopted. Sparky assured his mother that his angel would help. He said, "The angel will convince the adopting family to do the right thing." "The angel has already visited the family," he added.

When news of the five-year reunion hit the paper, the adopting family returned to the orphanage and offered to help in reuniting the family.

The subsequent years did not go without Sparky's constant companion being ever present. Decades later, Sparky remembers dozens more times when the angel kept him from danger and even death. Sparky says, "Without the angel active in my life, there were dozens of instances when I was only two seconds from eternity. We all have guardian angels. It's up to us whether or not we listen to them."

# TO PRAY
# OR NOT TO PRAY

**Do we even know how, or when or why?**

I often hear a person say, "I bought a ticket for the Mega Millions lottery tonight. I pray that I might win." It is ten o' clock at night, and the lottery game has already been played and the results announced. Why should prayer improve the odds of winning? The time for prayer would have been before the drawing took place. Praying after the results have already been announced certainly won't help.

I hear people say, "I hope my money came today." I pray that it did. If the mail has already been delivered and the check did not arrive, what good will prayer do?

I heard a man talking about his wife's car having a blowout and running into a cornfield. "My wife called and said she is ok. I pray the car was not damaged." The act has already transpired. If the car was damaged, praying is not going to undo the situation. The time for prayer would have been before the trip began.

Do we know when to pray? Do we know how to pray? Do we know why we should pray? From some of the comments I hear in casual conversation, I sometimes think not!

There is a time to pray and a way to pray. In addition to the times we pray by traditions that are inherent in our psyche, there is a time and way to utilize the power of prayer. Loosely prayed petitions and casual prayer are moot. Prayer should come from down within our soul. It should be meaningful and sincere; not carelessly cast upon the winds in "hopes" that prayer will help. Hope is a doubt, a negative aspect of prayer. We should pray or light a candle in total sincerity before, not after. We should pray regularly, not haphazardly. We should begin our day in prayer and end the evening in prayer and meditation. Prayer is the petitioning to the higher power, and meditation is the act of listening for the answer.

I recently had a person come to me in need of medical attention. The man said he needed a healing badly. I instructed him that a healing, although powerful and often brings immediate results, is not an excuse for not consulting a physician. His reply was that he could not afford to seek medical attention and his pride would not allow him to accept charity. I said a healing prayer as I would for anyone who seeks my help. I did it without thinking of any type of reward or thanks or payment. The power utilized in prayer comes from God and is not something that I alone possess. It is given freely and should be shared freely. The results of the healing prayer were almost instant. The changes in the man's physical and mental conditions changed so overwhelmingly that one would have his faith reaffirmed without doubt, both on the prayer and the one seeking aid.

Another person sought assistance in the form of a spiritual healing. The attention and focus of this healing was the same as the former with the exception of one very important fact. The only comment from the person seeking the healing was, "Wow, I certainly hope that works!" My immediate reply was, "Unless you have a more positive attitude, no amount of prayer will make a difference." Doubt is a very negative deterrent to any healing technique or any prayer, no matter how strong. Doubt can overcome the results of a healing or prayer and has more of a negative impact than the prayer can overcome. It was almost like the person didn't really want a healing and simply wanted the continued attention that he was getting.

When we go into our meditation chamber, we should enter in the security and knowledge that prayer and meditation will benefit us or the act or person for whom we are praying. The infinite power of the universe should be "thanked for the blessings that we have received and the blessing that we have yet to receive." It doesn't matter if we pray to God, Buddha, Allah or simply the infinite power of the universe. Our intentions must be sincere. We must do everything in our power to assist in the positive outcome of our prayer. If we are praying to overcome alcoholism, we certainly must make every effort on our part to stop drinking. By finishing our prayer and heading to the refrigerator for a six-pack, we are not exerting the efforts necessary on our part to cause the desired results. The law of cause and effect play an important role in prayer. We must consider this when we send our petitions to the infinite source of prayer. *Prayer without work, at least some type of work, is dead.*

We are all aware of the lessons we learn in the classes we take, the lectures and healings we witness at church, etc. When it comes down to the basics, we never seem to remember. Is it possible that we don't want to accept that which we know to be true? Is it possible we don't want to be spurned by our friends for what we believe and know to be fact? Perhaps it will take another century for us to come to the realization that many of our teachings have merit and warrant a second look. Yes, maybe another hundreds years will do the trick.

# MY DOG, THE PSYCHIC

In 1990, my brother was given an eighty-pound Heidelberg Shepherd by a local radio host. This was a show dog with hundreds of awards. We soon realized his degree of intelligence. Due to his size, he was called "Samson." He retrieved the mail shoved through the mail slot. He fetched the newspaper from the lawn. He picked up socks and dropped them in the laundry chute. If a towel fell to the floor, he promptly retrieved it. He only had to witness the door handle operation one time before he could open the door to go outside. He wiped his paws on a throw rug usually used by adults

One day in May of 1996, when I returned to the office, I saw Samson standing there whining with his front paws on the top of the gate. He didn't wait for me to close the gate before grabbing my sleeve and pulling me toward the door. I had seen enough Lassie re-runs to realize that something was wrong. When we got inside, Lyle was watching television as if nothing had happened.

A few hours later, Lyle complained of severe chest pains. He didn't want the exhibition of being "hauled off" by an ambulance. I backed the car out of the drive while Samson made a beeline to the car. The three of us headed for the hospital. Within five minutes, we were filling out admitting papers and discussing by-pass surgery. Both Lyle and I had thought the pain was simply a pulled muscle from a heavy workload the day before.

It was a couple of months before the work schedule returned to normal. Lyle was operating a large printing press, something he had done for decades without a scratch. Again, Samson tugged on my sleeve to get my attention and go inside.

I rushed inside and all seemed normal. The press was running smoothly as usual and no cause for concern. At that moment, the lights went out due to a power failure common in our neighborhood. The loss of power caused a piece of paper to become lodged between two of the rollers. As Lyle tried to retrieve the jammed paper, the power came back on severing his index finger. Samson was standing beside the press with the car keys between his teeth, and five minutes later, we were in the emergency room. The finger was successfully attached

The rest of the month went without incident. It was only three days into the next month when Samson came running to me with the car keys. I thought, "What now?" Everything seemed to be running smoothly. Nothing seemed out of the ordinary. Within minutes, the phone rang. It was the emergency room calling to inform me that another brother had just been admitted due to an industrial accident on his job.

The next few months seemed normal. We were returning to a regular routine when Samson brought the keys again. I waited to see what would happen. Nothing did! I returned the keys to my desk. He promptly brought them back. This went on for three days. I had been pampering my tooth until a more appropriate time to seek dental attention. Samson continued to bring the keys. Finally, the last time he brought the keys, my tooth was worse, so I gave him a treat and a pat on the head, and headed to the dentist. After the examination, the dentist gave me a blank stare. "I don't know how to tell you this," he said. "You don't have a toothache; I suspect you have throat cancer." A second and third opinion verified the diagnosis. I was admitted to Toledo Hospital for surgery. After surgery, Samson was constantly uneasy as I went through radiation treatments. He sat by my chair and slept at the foot of my bed until I was able to return to a normal routine.

Samson was my brother's dog; although to him, we were one. It was as though he was with both of us at the same time.

After my recovery, things seemed normal. I began to gain weight and eventually discontinued all doctor visits. The spiritual healings and prayers that I received from friends seemed to have better results than the thousands of dollars in medicine that I spent on a monthly basis.

Samson knew I was okay and my family looked on each day a lot easier. We knew that if he did not bring us the keys, everyone was safe.

Life became easier and Lyle and I had reached the point of thinking all was well, when Samson brought keys again. On a Monday, before I started to work, he brought the keys. On Tuesday he brought the keys again. Wednesday, when I went to the door, he did not bring them. He didn't even come to see me off to work. I was running late, so I ran in search of my keys. They were nowhere to be found. I went into the bedroom, and Samson was still at the foot of the bed. He was lying there lifeless with the keys still in his mouth. Once again, and for the last time, Samson's prediction was completely accurate. As I reached down to retrieve a steno pad that had been on my nightstand for years to record dreams, I noticed a faint muddy paw print ever so lovingly placed in the center of the page. Samson was gone.

# SUN WORSHIP

### Were the Ancients
### privy to hidden knowledge?

**B**eing recognized in Egypt and surrounding countries as a sun worshipper could possibly have a more mundane, yet beneficial meaning than we have been led to believe. While many schools of thought bend toward father sun and mother moon, there are those that believe there are more hidden beneficial icons than we have thought possible.

While most of the sun worshippers were of nobility, it stands to reason that they were given all the esoteric knowledge of the soothsayers, scribes and sachems of the day. As late as this century, we find many sun worshippers, especially in the Midwest.

Why is this practice still so prevalent, yet unknown to the majority of the population? Are there hidden or mystical or perhaps magical properties associated with the rays of the sun or the luminous glow of the moon?

It is an established fact that "ol' sol" acts as a purification agent on the earth as well as the air. The tremendous heat of the sun on the earth not only aids in cleansing of dead animals by contributing to decomposition, but also acts as a vitamin-inducing agent on the human body. It also aids in dispelling bodily toxins and in healing infections by contributing to the healing properties of abscesses. In addition, the sun covers them with a most powerful antibiotic, the salt from human perspiration. This act is much akin to the same effects as awarded us by a foot soak of many "over the counter" agents including Epsom Salt.

Many of the ancient sun worshippers, though considering the sun a god, highly regarded the moon as the wife of the sun, or a goddess. The same applies to the beneficial properties of the moon as that of the sun. The relaxing effects attributed to the moon are equally as harmonizing and beneficial to one's health as the powerful rays of the sun. Tranquility is the most prominent aspect awarded us by the moon. This awards us a time of peace and healing of our mental, physical and spiritual bodies, as well as comfort and consolation to the soul. We are affected by all actions around us. We heal better and faster when we laugh, when we meditate and when we sleep. The peaceful serenity of the moon plays an equal part in any recovery. When we sit in recluse, enjoying the silent rays of the moon, we are immune to the violent and furious activities of the day and place our spiritual self on the higher embodiment of the moon. If it worked for the ancients, who is to say it won't work today? They had wars, feast and famine, but they never had the dilemma of the twenty-first century. Food for thought? Maybe yes...maybe no!

# THE REALM OF POSSIBILITY LIES IN EACH OF US

    Joseph Rostenberry, an accomplished self-motivation teacher, lecturer and author was born in a small parish in Louisiana. He frequently visited the grave of Marie LeVeau. He was a local at the community readers and psychics, in search of answers about his unusual and unique birthmarks.

    Joseph was born with noticeable piercing of both ears as well as his nose. This brought severe and constant ridicule from his peers during adolescence and junior high school. The names like "sissy" and "mamma's boy" were commonplace and a condition to which he grew to expect and accept as a fact of life on a daily basis. As an adult, he tried to hide the piercing with women's make-up as they became more accented as he aged. The holes became larger even after maturity, and Joseph was desperate to find answers. He felt he needed someone, anyone, to give him an acceptable answer, no matter how ridiculous it may be. The sarcasm and mockery was reaching the point that it almost reached insanity. Unless he found answers and found them quick, Joseph felt that he would possibly do something unforgivable, the unpardonable sin.

    Joseph, on a recent business trip to Toledo stopped in the *Body, Mind & Spirit Publishing Office.* He had recently picked up a copy at a spiritualist retreat near

Cassadaga, a spiritualist camp in Florida. An article we printed on birthmarks intrigued him.

Since we make every effort to be totally impartial and play no favorites, we gave him a computer printout of every listing that we had received for our future-printing edition of the *New Age Directory*. After going over each listing we have received, we agreed on ten listings that might be able to assist in his dilemma.

After his three-day business seminar concluded, Joseph reserved his final night for contacting psychics from our list. He made arrangements for four psychics to visit his suite at a downtown hotel. One of those contacted was a former member of the First Spiritualist Church on Western Avenue in Toledo. A séance was conducted in Joseph's hotel suite in a last and desperate attempt to discover the meaning of his perplexing predicament.

On his way to the airport the following day, Joseph revisited our office and explained that the Toledo psychic from the First Spiritualist Church had satisfactorily explained the unusual birthmarks as being the trappings of royalty as an Amazon Chief over a hundred years ago. The gold rings that adorned each piercing were a sign of prestige and a station in life, and they were a symbol of the utmost respect. Joseph decided that he could accept this, and this would turn his life around. "It is extremely difficult to attempt to motivate others when I cannot motivate myself," he said with misty eyes.

Although the height of my exuberance was the fact that he had found closure in his birthmarks harassment, I was overjoyed when he told me that the four psychics invited to his hotel were very sensible about payment. The charges per person ranged from fifty dollars to a hundred dollars, but the reader from the First Spiritualist Church asked only for cab fare. This reminds me of the dedication that we all afforded our clients decades ago, when most readers were afraid to speak. In the late sixties, there appeared to be a "witch-hunt" in Toledo and psychics and readers were encouraged to purchase a license. There were a few who supposedly did purchase this license, but there were many underground readers and psychics that opposed this action.

We were thrilled to have him visit us; and more important than his success, we were happy to see that support was still available in the Toledo area and that helping others was more important than the almighty dollar.

# The Doctor Within

For hundreds of years, we have spurned that which we do not understand. Over a century ago, my grandmother, a sainted woman, was ostracized because she used the knowledge of her grandmother to perform healing rites utilizing only the herbs, berries, barks and roots that were readily available.

We often wonder where the original laws of healing took root. Did they spew forth from the belly of mother earth? Who were the original healers, spiritual advisors and the rest of the members who went forth performing healings without ever hanging a shingle and placing a monetary price on knowledge and adhering to the rules inherent in most men? Did they receive their knowledge strictly by trial and error? I think not. Much of the knowledge they received from their parents and grandparents. Great, but where did they get it?

The intuitive factor that is inherent in us all is possibly our greatest teacher. Even in these latter days, long after the Stone Age, the Metal Age, the introduction of slaves and the proclamation freeing them, we still refuse to recognize the abilities inherent in us all. While it is true that some are more advanced than others, we still have that spark either dormant or fuel fed, anxiously awaiting its re-birth.

During my bout with cancer, my first visit was to a healer who did not gloat over a piece of paper displayed on a wall with less than a dollar's worth of glass protecting it. The healer I went to only had a high school education. Perhaps I had a "telephone book of healers" at my disposal. In fact, I did. I had the last *New Age Directory* printed a few years ago. Although many of those listed had moved, died or got the "holy ghost" and became more sanctimonious than thou, I still had a select few which were known by me to be viable Christian healers.

It was an accident that I discovered the cancer. I thought I merely had a toothache. I visited my dentist for a possible abscess. The shocking news that I received from the dentist would have knocked the average bird off his perch. He sent me to a specialist for a second opinion. I decided I needed a third opinion and opted for a fourth. They all told me the same thing, "Immediate surgery was imperative." I did not want a young whelp still wet behind the ears cutting on me. I wanted a seasoned practitioner with a few years experience under his belt. After the fourth opinion, I chose possibly the youngest surgeon in Toledo to perform the operation. Why? I asked myself that same question over and over.

Although I was told the need for immediate surgery was paramount, I still listened to my "spirit doctor within." I visited the best healers I knew. I went to a healer in Cleveland, Ohio, the First Spiritualist Church, Toledo, Ohio; MESA Metaphysical Association of Toledo, Ohio, as well as my own spirit doctor who constantly gave me weird, unbelievable remedies, poultices and exercises to perform on a daily basis.

The young surgeon told me that it was imperative that I have the surgery immediately, but I put it off until I could consult "my spirit doctors." Since I am not a medical doctor; I will not disclose the awful tasting gargles and herbs that I used. After two weeks of healings and home remedies, my surgeon was amazed at the improvement. He could not explain the drastic improvement in the cancerous growths, other than possibly my body was fighting off the disease.

America is not ready to accept the fact that each of us has a doctor within, telling us how and what to do for a healthy lifestyle. In the event we do recognize the fact and possibly tell others, we are considered candidates for the funny farm. We don't consider the health of our forefathers or perhaps the health of the Native American. Where were the surgeons then? The settlers on the American plains often consulted the "wise woman" or the community healer. The doctors were often few and far between. I admit the air was cleaner and the food contained fewer toxins. Yet, we still refuse to accept the fact that we are our own worst enemies.

One particular flu season brought on more strains than any in recent memory. It reared its ugly head in my household as well. Everyone in the house became extremely ill. Only one member of the family received the recommended flu shot. This made no difference. He became extremely ill anyway. He returned to the doctor for antibiotics and cough suppressants. It appeared that we were passing the bug back and forth for over ten weeks. We would improve slightly for a couple of days, but then the next day brought full measure back.

Due to constant "programming" by television, radio and newspapers, we blamed our illness on the flu. This is one of the reasons we are unable to ward off most ailments. We are "programmed" to accept the illness with open arms. This is not unlike the psychological programming utilized by the Japanese on prisoners of war, as well as the programming of Viet Nam prisoners. This "programming" also worked in my household. It was well into the second month of coughing, runny nose, watering eyes and chronic pain, before someone asked me, "What does your inner doctor say?" It is extremely difficult in these latter days to remember to practice what we preach. That question really hit home, as I had not even considered the feasibility of self-induced ailments.

A special meeting was called in our sanctuary. After a basic relaxation technique, we began our meditation to consult our own "private doctors." In less than five minutes, we were told we had the equivalent to Legionnaire's Disease. I was confused. I couldn't imagine how my whole family could have contracted anything even remotely similar to Legionnaire's Disease. My brother reminded me that we had installed a new furnace only three months earlier. The ailments were coming from germs that had accumulated in the furnace filters during a long storage. At one time, the filter had been saturated by about four inches of water during a heavy rain. We were advised to replace the filter, and spray the unit with bleach, as well as the complete bathroom and all sinks. In addition, all bed linen was cleaned with bleach, beds and entire household sprayed with antiseptic. Twenty-four hours later, the entire household displayed no more signs of the flu.

# THE LAST CRY

Pat Ramon and I had been friends since the late sixties. We partied together, went to socials together, visited each other often and were there for each other through thick and thin.

I had always been able to sense sickness in anyone who came close to me. It was always the smell of death. It reminded me of a person confined to a sick room without bathing for weeks.

It was around 1979, when I became conscious of that same faint scent coming from Patty. We were still relatively young at that time, so I dismissed the thought. Normally, I would have meditated on the situation to ascertain whether or not I could send healing energy to the ailment. I was never one to confront anyone about an illness. If the subject ever arose, I volunteered a healing prayer.

Later that year, Patty was admitted to Riverside Hospital in Toledo for possible Tuberculosis. She underwent exploratory surgery, and it was concluded to be a false alarm. We were thankful for the results but a year later, the fragrance became more noticeable. It appeared that no one noticed it but me.

As the condition persisted, our outings became fewer and fewer until finally they were practically nonexistent. By the end of 1999, we seldom ventured out. Patty lived alone and yearned for constant companionship. It was at this time she went to the Humane Society in search for a companion. She found a Chihuahua and immediately fell in love with it. She called her "Tiny," and it immediately became the main focus in her life.

As time went on, her symptoms became worse and she eventually resorted to the use of a hospital walker just to maneuver around the house. She began to lose about five pounds of weight each week, yet the doctors did not give her any satisfactory explanation.

The first part of 2005, Tiny showed signs of a tumor on her stomach. Patty, being the doting "mom" rushed her to the vet. A battery of tests showed the tiny pooch to have early stages of lung cancer and a tumor in the lower intestine. The vet cautioned against surgery. "The little tyke will live a couple of years longer if we don't operate," he said. "Surgery would only aggravate the condition." Holding back the tears, Patty picked up her little angel, and I drove her back home. It was at this point that I noticed the same "scent" around Tiny. The dog seemed to lose all energy and range of motion. It just wanted to lie around and occasionally exercise bodily functions. That same week, I received a call from her neighbor informing me that Patty's phone had been busy all day. This was strange so I immediately rushed over to find her lying on the floor. She had been there all day. I called for an ambulance; and after it left, I took Tiny home with me. The sluggishness remained with the tiny pooch. I simply attributed it to old age. The next few days, Patty remained under guarded care at the hospital and Tiny stayed with me. Each day it seemed that Tiny had more and more problems motivating and even the simplest task was difficult. When I visited the hospital that day, the same symptoms were evident with Patty. It was as though her tiny companion was experiencing the same maladies as her caregiver. Over the next few days, I maintained constant vigilance on the dog and took several pictures and pages of notes.

One Friday morning as I arose, I noted the small canine lying on her side and moaning as if in severe pain. I immediately called the hospital to discover that Patty had fallen. She had attempted to slide out of bed and severely fractured her hip. This required immediate surgery and resulted in several pins being inserted into the hip. She was transferred to a nursing rehabilitation center just outside Toledo. There she would receive physical therapy and learn to walk with a cane. The regimen was strenuous and a three-time daily ritual.

Tiny visited the nursing home on a regular basis and soon started to lose weight. Although her eating habits did not change, the tiny pooch lost about a pound a week. The vet said nothing was wrong with her other than old age and the aforementioned ailments. He could not explain the sudden loss of weight. My next visit to the rehabilitation center, I witnessed a much thinner Patty than ever before. She too, had started losing weight at the rate of about ten pounds a week. The doctors had no explanation. I asked for a second opinion of her condition and the results were shocking. Patty had inoperable lung cancer and no one had told her. This explained her constant loss of weight and failing health.

I contacted Linda Dix, a noted Toledo psychic and asked for advice. Linda told me that Patty needed assurance that her tiny companion would be taken care of. "She needs comfort and assurance," Linda added. "I am saddened to say more."

During my evening visit, Patty was still coherent but could only speak in a whisper. Patty asked me to move into her house and take care of her baby. I was stunned, but agreed. "I will move into your house and take care of Tiny the rest of her life," I assured her as I gave her a kiss on the cheek. "Good," she replied. "That is what I wanted to hear."

I left the center and returned home only to receive a waiting phone call to return to the Center. Upon my arrival, my expectations rang true. Patty passed on. Although I had a comfortable home, I moved into Patty's house with her dog. Tiny immediately regained her health and became active again. She lived another seven years and died of old age.

# THE EUPHORIA OF SALVATION

### (The joys of being saved)

**M**artin Taborelli came to Toledo from Skowhegan, Maine. He was a construction worker and electrician. For the past few months, he had been unable to find a job to support his wife and children. He had been to the doctor for nerves and was eating pills like candy. He thought he was at the end of his rope and suicide was not out of the question. His life was a total nightmare. Everything he touched would collapse. Bills and the possibility of his ailing wife leaving him consumed his mind. His mind was in shambles. He found the *Body, Mind and Spirit News* in the phone book and called our office. I was on the phone with him for over an hour.

The next day, he paid us a visit. I gave him a current copy of the paper. After coffee and homemade sweets that many of our readers dropped off for Christmas, he said farewell.

The first week of January brought Martin back to our office. He reminded me that if any of our psychics helped solve his problem, he would allow us to print the article. "I am proud to give you my story," he boasted.

After reading the newspaper and seeing all the psychics listed, Taborelli said it was like a breath of fresh air after coming out of a siege of smog. He contacted various psychics in the metropolitan Toledo area and was told basically the same thing. He had to change his attitude before changing his life and securing a satisfactory position. "It was like I had to be saved, first" he said. Martin who was baptized a Catholic had leaned slightly toward the pagan faith and was torn between the two.

He struggled for days trying to change his attitude. That was when he watched the movies, *Sister Act* and *Sister Act II*, with Whoopi Goldberg and Kathy Najimy. The two movies struck such a positive note that Taborelli said he could not get them out of his mind. The first movie, *Sister Act* contained a boogie-woogie beat inside a cathedral, which radiated outside pulling others in to hear the angelic music. The second movie, *Sister Act II* contained a high school group song with a young African American boy in the lead singing "Oh Happy Days." The first few days after, Taborelli had boogie-woogie on his mind. The high "C" note of "Oh Happy Days" consumed him. During these few days, Taborelli says that his attitude was totally positive. He didn't drop anything, use any profanity, or cast any aspersions. His day was filled with smiles and good words for everyone.

After the episodes with the Whoopi Goldberg movies, Taborelli was then guided to the Goodwill Spiritualist Church in Walbridge, Ohio. It was after his visit there that he could not forget the circle in the chapel where they sang, "Let there be Peace on Earth and Let it Begin with Me" that culminated the service. This song, he carried in his heart and mind for the next few days.

Taborelli tells us that it is not necessary to be baptized with water to be saved. The positive attitude of a few good people is sometimes all it takes to bring a man from the brink of despair to the heights of illumination. Taborelli has since obtained gainful employment and gotten his life back together. He attributes this to a simple phone call to the *Body, Mind and Spirit News*. We are pleased that we were allowed to be a small part of this transformation.

# 2012 - A Mayan Transformation?

**F**east or famine? The Mayans, like modern man believed the world was destroyed before and will be destroyed again. This belief has now become more apparent than ever before. We are making too many demands on our environment and our planet. Food is depleting, while the population is exploding at an alarming rate. Unemployment is skyrocketing due to sending jobs overseas and other ridiculous conditions. Of course our "leaders" always know best!

We are now witnessing wars and rumors of wars, which have been foretold since the beginning of time. The homeless are an increasing concern and out of control. We are sending rockets to the moon as well as other such attempts to explore and understand our vast universe. The jets we see daily, the pollution and radiation flushed into our national water system, the cancerous fish that are becoming so common in the fishing industry; the fact is that the world is slowly being poisoned. Death at this rate is inevitable. The possibility of man sustaining himself without the supermarket, the utility companies, and travel, are rapidly becoming less and less assured.

The first thing one must consider is the power of the mind and the inner sanctum as being one of the most powerful machines on earth. This is paramount as we embark upon these latter days of uncertainty. World conditions are crumbling, and many of the things we always took for granted will no longer be available if we continue this destructive path.

The American government and others around the world are less assured of themselves than they have been in decades. Small businesses are filing bankruptcy at an all time high. What do we have to fall back on? Greed begets greed. Are we heading to a point where we will kill for a loaf of bread?

The Native Americans teach us a totally different philosophy - a thought-provoking lifestyle with considerably more merit than our current system of "taking from the poor and giving to the rich."

Before the days of Hitler and Mussolini, even before the pyramids, we had basically the same philosophy. It has only been the past few decades since the surfacing of thought seekers like Edgar Cayce, Harold Sherman, Sol Lewis, and our own local thought groups, that the select few can see past the ends of their noses.

Churches, psychics, teachers, healers, etc., are showing us the alternative avenues of thought and existence. Now, as in days of old, there are simply too many road signs, and the maps still don't tell us how to get from here to there.

The Mayan calendar points to a great change in 2012. Could it be? Most of the ancients seemed to have an invisible telephone line to a vast storehouse of knowledge.

Where do our telephone lines lead today? It is up to the individual within each of us to tell the operator that we were given a wrong number and wish to be reconnected with the right one.

In October 2007, oil reached $94.80 a barrel. Iran is planning nuclear power stations, which will result in nuclear weapons. Pakistan already has nuclear capabilities and hiding rebels in their border towns. This will lead to Al Qaida attacking nuclear power stations in Pakistan. They will then have nuclear weapons to threaten the United States and Israel. A nuclear attack on Israel will send deadly fallout around the globe. That will start World War III, the deadliest war in history. Millions will die. Then it will be too late.

# The Faith of a Grain of Mustard

Faith plays an important role in our everyday life, work, friends, and religious practices. We often associate "faith" and "belief," as one and the same. There is one remarkable difference. With our belief, we can believe in our government and we can have faith in it. With belief, we can possibly consider its safe assurance of a sound economy. Ha! That was a poor example. We can also believe it is sound. Without being an ever-seeing, all-knowing entity, who are we to say what condition the government is actually in? We know the structure is on extremely thin ice abroad, and there are those who will empathize with that belief here at home.

Once upon a time there was a great story being told that I would be able to retire and the government would send me a check every month to pay my bills. If
I got sick and couldn't work; the government would still send me a check to pay my bills. Sound familiar? Recently I received a printed form from the government telling me that I was not eligible to receive anything in the event that I could no longer work. It seems that there are certain things called "points" based on the amount of money that one pays in during their work life.

Of course, I could still retire and get that fabulous check. Now, that fabulous check would probably rent me one room with community bath accommodation. Don't think about having cable TV, as that will then be a luxury that I wouldn't be able to afford. All my early years were embedded with this fairytale and I believed it to be true and had faith in the assurance I would be taken care of in my golden years. Well, with the Social Security situation in its present condition, my faith has faltered. My belief has been smashed upon the jagged rocks.

In my spiritual life, my belief and faith still run hand-in-hand. It is written that the faith of a mustard seed can cause a mountain to be moved from this point to another point. Does this mean that the mountain can actually change locations? Or, does it simply mean that a mountain of sin can be dispersed. The tiny mustard seed, hardly the size of a tip of a match, must have some powerful "mo-jo" if it can do all that. That is not to say how much space that faith requires to fill a mustard seed.

The flight from Egypt with Moses is a perfect example of how faith can reach its peak only to collapse the very next minute. Miracle after miracle was required to reinforce the people's faith. The very second things went awry, the faith crumbled to dust. Another miracle was required to peak their faith again. When all was said and done, it took forty years before the weary travelers reached their destination. Even to this day, their faith is still tested. It is not something that everyone has.

Faith is required. It is a 'must' in this day and age. The world is crumbling down upon us, the economy is failing, unemployment is rampant, and hunger abounds from sea to sea as well as around the world. It has even reached the point that the United States has to pay foreign countries millions of dollars so they will not attack our allies or us. If faith was so important centuries ago, is it any less important today?

After a recent bout with cancer, I knew that faith was the only thing that would bring me through. My doctor said without the operation, I had less than six months as the cancer was rapidly approaching my brain. With reluctance, I had the surgery along with all the radiation treatments, intravenous feeding, agonizing pain and the like. I took on the copious, somewhat insurmountable problems, with faith. My weight immediately dropped from two hundred thirty pounds to a straggly one hundred thirty-five. It was faith coupled with anger as to why I contracted cancer in the first place. Faith kept me alive, but it was the anger that actually gave me the energy and determination to continue.

Before I had completed the radiation treatment, I said goodbye to three of my friends who died from the same type of operation. I remember pounding my theories of faith into one of them. A friend of over twenty years, it was apparent that faith was lacking. He continually told me he had faith but his comment of, "I hope I make it through another day," was one of the points leading to the total decline of his faith. I witnessed his steady downfall that took approximately six weeks before he completely lost all signs of faith and gave up. At that point, "hope" wasn't even an option.

Faith without work is dead. Prayer without work is dead. Even though I had a strong belief, I could not let "hope" enter the picture, as that would detract from the faith and the *"I know"* that I had already instilled within every cell of my being. Prayer without work is dead. I could pray to win the lottery. Without work, even the smallest amount, must come into play. How can I win if I don't buy a ticket? How can I win if I don't work to obtain the money for the ticket? Some form of work is mandatory.

One simple way to assist in maintaining faith is through positive thinking and daily affirmations. The use of a candle can greatly enhance the positive flow, by reminding us every time we make visual contact with the candle. Prayer in any format is essential to maintaining a serene state of mind so necessary in nurturing faith.

Who can say how much faith a mustard seed can hold and how much faith it takes to materialize that which you desire in your life? At least without faith, you won't get it. Faith is the driving factor that leads us all in the right direction to achieve our goals. Faith is that which manifests itself in our everyday life. Faith in our self, friends, business relationships, health, and even down to the tiniest fiber of our body, is heir apparent to our ultimate survival.

# STICKS AND STONES DOES NOT A FRIENDSHIP BREAK

Rumors and gossip seem to run rampant by some who for some unscrupulous or unknown reason are innocent pawns who have been handed down second or third generation gossip. With each passing of slander, the story grows like Pinocchio's nose.

This trend became more prominent after Psychic Sunday, a special affair that was held to promote unity and foster and perpetuate a better understanding of what the metaphysical community is all about. However, the fear factor induced by a select few prompted some to completely drop out of sight after years of dedication to healing and metaphysical study and practice.

There are those who call students and practitioners of the psychic sciences, wizards, warlocks, weirdoes, charlatans, and the list goes on and on. With each passing of the story, it seems to be embellished to somewhat of a greater degree than when it was passed down.

It does not matter what one's religion is as long as the masses work for the common good of the community, whether the metaphysical community, Wiccan community, Jewish community or atheist. The name-calling and mud slinging seems to continue even long after the death of the world's greatest psychic, Jesus Christ. He was not only the alleged son of God, but a teacher, healer, psychic, and yes, student. We are all on the pathway of learning to improve ourselves, to become greater and more proficient in our chosen field. The countless healers in the world vary as the hairs on our head. It doesn't matter what technique the physician utilizes to accomplish the healing. The only thing that matters is the simple fact that someone in pain is being helped.

The thousands who practice the arts of healing, divining, and any other aspect of metaphysics not requiring a four to twelve year sheet of paper received from some building comprised of mortar and stone is on the rise. I receive dozens of letters each month telling me of the benefits received from prayer and the many articles resulting in the regaining of one's faith. Too many people fall by the wayside, simply because a single narrow-minded person slaps them in the face with constant bombardment of trash and putrid accusations. Too many never recover from the scars inflicted on their psyche. Some will eventually recover, but many of the excellent prospective healers will never regain the trust in their fellow man that they once had.

In over fifty years of study, I have witnessed and experienced many of these trashy remarks made by acquaintances and close friends. Some accusations come from religious leaders who don't deserve the ten-cent piece of paper that entitles them to be called "Reverend." Ministers are supposed to help all those that come to them, not slap them in the face and slander their beliefs, regardless of what they may be. Rumors flow like molasses in some instances, in an attempt to break up friendships that have been welded together for decades.

I feel it is my job to make a statement, and that is exactly what I intend to do! I have been consumed of late by the reports that I am hearing about someone being a friend to someone in the Wiccan religion or someone that does not totally believe in all the Bible has to say! This is a crock! The Bible was written by man, and I know of not one in this life or a past life that is infallible. Reports on many syndicated channels are bringing to light many of the discrepancies of the Bible that we had shoved down our throats from childhood. Does it not stand to reason that if Christ could sup with those less pure, then who is to call the kettle black today? Simply because someone is a friend with those of another faith, even Wiccan, does not mean that a spell is imposed on that person and they must bend to every whim. We are our own individual person and we only have to answer for our own actions, regardless of the consequences.

We don't have to hide our associations with others. That is one of the few things that we can honor in these latter days. Let the trash fall where it may. The actions don't warrant the breath it takes to exert it.

# HELL ON EARTH

Belief in a fiery burning hell has tormented my life from earlier days when my parents kept shoving a horned being with a long tail breathing fire, down my throat. I was at the point that I wouldn't sneeze unless I was sure no one was present. I didn't want anyone to get the germs. That would send me straight to hell, "just a poppin," as was the favorite expression of my sainted mother. She was consumed by the supposed devil hovering over her shoulder.

A more sainted person than my mother never lived. Her actions were inherited from her parents, who were married for over seventy-five years and never uttered a cross word to each other. When my grandmother died at the age of ninety-nine, she had never been to the hospital or even a casual visit to the doctor. She became ill one day and immediately began her regimen of raspberry roots and birch bark teas, mustard plasters and a daily infusion of dandelion leaves to her diet. A daily ritual of raw ginger and black cherries seemed to bring her back to her normal routine, but it was short lived. One day in the middle of a humid summer day, she did not awake. She was taken to the hospital about forty-five miles away. She was revived only to pass to her eternal reward the next day.

She was laid out in a wooden casket in her living room where friends came to pay their respects. My grandfather was by her side the entire time, resigning from life. At the cemetery, reality finally set in, and he emitted a single tear which was only noticed by me. We made efforts to comfort him, but at my early age, I was afraid my efforts went in vain. I loved him dearly, as he and my grandmother were the closest to saints that I had, or will ever see in this lifetime. He went home immediately after the funeral and went to bed. He never took food or water; he only lay there contemplating his hour. This took seven days during which time he did not sleep; he only prayed for his wife and that the Lord would soon take him. He was 101 years old and finally closed his eyes in peace, assured of a place in heaven.

I lived with my grandparents from my early teens until shortly before graduation. During that time, I learned of heaven and hell and the do's and don'ts required for admission. I often reflect on their words but now look upon hell in a totally new context. I no longer regard it as a fiery furnace where I will burn until the end of time. I don't worry about some horned freak prodding me with a blazing pitchfork. In fact, I don't even believe in him anymore. In my opinion, those who wrote the books of the Bible also wrote and invented Satan as a fear tactic to keep the multitudes in line. Times were hard in those days and possibly this might have been a form of insurance. My actions and deeds will determine if I die in peace with a sinless soul, or be consumed by foul deeds assuring a tormented mind at death.

The exodus from Egypt is a good example. The earlier days brought only joy and high expectations; where after those joys, it turned to despair, jealousy, envy and greed. They lost their religion on countless occasions and reverted to the ancient ways. They all knew of the Ten Commandments as brought down from Mount Sinai. As they were being introduced by Moses, the people had already lost their faith...again! Considering the sanctimonious believers of those days who continually lost their faith and supposedly gained it back when things went better, who are we and what are we to believe? Without faith in some form or fashion, this would be a sad place to live.

In many instances, we recall the teachings of the Ten Commandments. In the very next sentence, we recall instances where they were already being broken. It seems that even in biblical days, it was okay to break a commandment when that action was directed toward someone else who had broken one. The most commonly broken commandment was "Thou shalt not kill." It seems that it was okay to kill a woman by stoning her if she broke the adultery commandment. It was okay to sacrifice a child to encourage a fruitful harvest. Even to this day, the descendants of the exodus from Egypt are breaking the most popular commandment on a daily basis. It has been that way for thousands of years, and it will continue to be that way until some fool blows us to kingdom come. Then, it won't make much difference. The direction we are heading now points to the inevitable.

The state of the nation in these latter days convinces me more and more that hell, as we regard it, is here and now! The commandments are now a mere haze in the life that we are born into. We don't have to worry about going to hell. We live in it. Even the pope has alluded to the fact that hell is a state of our mind upon death. It seems that the state of mind upon transition is the determining factor as to whether we die in peace to be reincarnated in a higher plane, or if we die in shame and doomed to relive *this* hellish life again.

If this plane is hell, who in their right mind would want to live it again? Faith! Anyone who doesn't have it or has lost it would be better off to look for it. It can be found or recovered simply by reading a book.

The rule of the day in ancient times was for God to curse the wicked and destroy them. It was the strong arm of God for Joshua to destroy Jericho. It was an easy task to clear up the corruption in Sodom and Gomorrah. Now we depend upon tornadoes, hurricanes, volcanoes and uncontrollable fires to cleanse what used to be taken care of in the blink of an eye.

Whether my ideas of hell have merit or not, it is rapidly becoming a fact of life. The political structure is tumbling, the economy will take a miracle to rebound, and disease and corruption are on an ever increasing spiral. Whether or not hell is an actual place where we will burn for eternity, it seems as though this world is heading that way in leaps and bounds. Is there a possibility of a 380 degree turn-around? Time will eventually reveal the outcome.

**The world no longer respects *"values."* The emphasis is now focused on "<u>VALUE</u>."**

# The Law of Three
## Or
## (What You Dish Out...)

The person relaying this story has requested that we use anonymity when referring to him or his position. We have agreed in order to commit his story to paper. We will call him Frenchie.

Frenchie knows only too well the law of cause and effect or the law of three, "Do unto others, harm no one, my will be done." He attributes the following positives to his efforts at a Psychic Sunday occasion at the First Spiritualist Church in Toledo, Ohio.

Frenchie was a regular at the church for some time. He had become disgruntled at the metaphysical community a few years prior due to the considerable amount of politics and dissension among the members. "It is not only one group, but many of the metaphysical organizations," he says. "It is like many individuals are on a power struggle and impervious to anyone's feelings or opinions or suggestions." Frenchie says he was compelled to assist with Psychic Sunday in order to regain his faith. "I have a very strong faith," he said. "I have always believed in a higher power and I definitely believe in *"as you sow, so shall you reap."* Frenchie has always believed that what you send out will return to you threefold, both negative and positive. It has been evident since that Psychic Sunday, in every aspect. Frenchie was a "behind the scene" volunteer for the award ceremony and never wanted to be in the limelight or have his name mentioned. We were proud to have him as a volunteer, as this is a facet of the metaphysical world that had been lacking.

When someone volunteers for a project, we should not look a gift horse in the mouth. "This is just something I had to do," Frenchie said. "The last time I was at a psychic function, the message I received was what we commonly refer to as a 'tube sock.' One size fits all. I actually felt more depressed after I left the event than before I went in. I am not referring to any group in particular," he added. "As a matter of fact, it wasn't a church at all. It was one of many functions that Toledo hosted a couple of years ago. Lately it seems as though Toledo is on the cutting edge. A lot of positive seeds have been sown lately, and I simply wanted to be a part of the growth process that nourishes the great change."

Frenchie admits to usually brandishing a negative outlook and is frequented by bad luck, bad health, and a myriad of travesties. "I simply must return to my former way of thinking." This was the trail leading back to sanity and a positive atmosphere encompassing his everyday life.

The day following the church function, Frenchie decided he needed a vacation and planned on heading to Florida the following day. After packing his bag, he discovered a number of problems with his car: no horn, radiator fan bad, and a couple of other discouraging problems, all demanding immediate attention. After surveying the problems plaguing him at this juncture, he decided to cancel his trip and headed back to his office with his suitcase. At this time, one of the attendees at Psychic Sunday was walking into the office at the same time.

After a bit of idle chatter, Frenchie was asked if he was just getting back from vacation. "No," he said. "The car is acting up and I am afraid to go." "Perhaps I can help," was the reply from the gentleman that Frenchie had only recently met. The man looked at the car and told Frenchie that emergency repairs could be made within a few minutes. The man went to a neighborhood junkyard and came back with a five-dollar part that made temporary repairs to the horn. Frenchie decided the radiator fan would make it to Florida and back. He repacked his car and took off.

When Frenchie reached Florida, he soon found himself in a twenty-mile traffic jam. He had a blowout on the rear of the car. A Florida State Trooper came by and changed the tire. (No, this is not a fairytale.) After getting back on the road, he had another blowout on the other side of the car. At that time, it was after midnight, no spare tire, nothing open, and no recourse. The cell phone did not work in a dead area. Within a few minutes, another Florida State Trooper stopped and offered aid. The trooper drove Frenchie almost thirty miles to a hotel and had his car towed to a local garage for next day repairs. The following day Frenchie asked the office manager to call a taxi to return to his car. The motel owner offered to drive him and would accept no pay. Upon returning to the garage where the car was towed, both tires on the back were changed and the spare was put back in the trunk. The garage just happened to be having a tire sale with 50% off and free installation.

The next day, Frenchie went to the I-95 flea market just outside of Daytona Beach. The car started to overheat, so he promptly pulled over to the side of the road. Much to his surprise, there was a junkyard only a few feet away. He went into the junkyard and inquired as to the possibility of acquiring a fan blade. He was told that they only had one car in the yard that would be suitable. The car had just been brought in with a wrecker. There was no radiator fan in it. Frenchie, in desperation decided to check out the yard anyway, just in case something could be found. If nothing else, his car would cool down and he could make it a few more miles heading back to his motel or perhaps to another garage. When the Frenchie found the car the manager had told him about, his inspection verified the manager's statement. There was no radiator fan; but upon closer inspection, he discovered a fan already removed, and in the back seat. Anxiously trying to beat an impending summer thundershower, he raced back to the office with the fan. The junkyard manager told him that if it had already been taken off, apparently someone had already purchased it and brought it back because it didn't work. Frenchie opted to take it anyway, and the manager only asked for $5 and offered to take it back if it didn't work. Frenchie hastened to remove the fan from his car and soon discovered that it had only been held in place by two screws and an "insert bracket" on the bottom. He installed the fan in less than three minutes and was back on the road. The fan was in perfect condition.

After spending a week on the beach soaking up sun, visiting the local attractions, and mailing postcards, Frenchie began his two-day jaunt back to Toledo.

Upon returning to Toledo, he discovered that his furnace had bit the dust. He remembered seeing an ad in a newspaper. The ad was for a handyman. Frenchie had a furnace in his garage that he had recently removed from a rental property. The handyman gave him a quote of three hundred dollars. Frenchie was short on funds and had to decline. The following day, the handyman came back in and offered to install the furnace in the old-fashion "barter" system. This was acceptable and the installation began. The handyman encountered numerous problems with the furnace resulting in a three- day ordeal. Frenchie was afraid the handyman would charge him for the extra time as the original plan was for a "one day" installation. When the furnace was installed, the handyman only asked for the cost of parts. After this three-day ordeal, the furnace still refused to operate properly. Since the handyman was not an electrician, he could not get the unit working properly. After three days, Frenchie told him that he would call an electrician. The handyman still refused payment. Frenchie did offer him a small stipend, which would have been inconsiderate for the handyman to refuse.

Frenchie called a furnace man and was informed that it would be two days before he could make a service call. Frenchie said he knew the repairman would be over the following day. "Things were simply on too much of a positive trend for anything else," he said. Sure enough, the following day shortly after noon, the furnace man walked into the office. This complex task of tracing the dozens of wires in the furnace promised to be a two-day job.

There were two repairmen working on the furnace at one time. The following day, the repairman returned with another assistant. The initial service call was one hundred twenty five dollars. Frenchie expected the same amount the following day. After the repairs were done, the repairman replaced the vent on the roof and made other repairs to the furnace, which had not even been discussed. At this time, Frenchie expected the repair bill to be in excess of three hundred dollars. After the completion of the job, the furnace man said, "I would like to barter with you on something I need. You can pay for parts, and I will barter for the labor." This was a totally unexpected surprise. Frenchie immediately agreed. Although the barter still cost money, it was far less than the three hundred dollars he expected to pay.

While in Florida, Frenchie noticed his car began to smoke excessively. He took it to a garage in Daytona Beach. He was told that the repairs needed would run in excess of eight hundred dollars. The quote was outrageous, as is the case in most repairs these days. Frenchie elected to baby the car home and dispose of it. It was an older car but in excellent shape, no rust, no dents.

Again, the same man that had repaired the horn and offered insurmountable free advice on the needed repairs came back into the office. "How's the car running?" was his first comment. Frenchie told him of his dilemma. "I am currently between jobs," the man said. "I will be happy to do the repairs for you. All you have to do is pay for parts and a few dollars to tide me over until my next job." Again, the law of cause and effect; the law of three is a most powerful tool in these latter days.

Inflation, outrageous insurance fees, ridiculous and outrageous gas price gouging, high prices for food, entertainment, etc., rapidly eats up the general weekly paycheck. This was too good to be true.

While in Florida, Frenchie utilized most of his time with his favorite pastime. Frenchie loves to go to auctions, flea markets, and visit thrift stores. He had purchased a few collectibles as well as a computer. When we experienced a power blackout a few weeks prior, his computer suffered a power surge rendering it totally useless. Now he had a computer better than the one he lost.

Among the things he bought at an auction were an antique anniversary clock from Germany and a beautiful hand-carved wall clock. The wall clock sold immediately to a clock collector. A newspaper advertiser purchased the anniversary clock for his wife as an anniversary present. The dedicated husband had forgotten the anniversary. He called Frenchie about nine o'clock, hours after closing. He was in the market for that perfect anniversary gift. What could be more natural for a perfect ending to a perfect example of the law of three?

May you always experience only the most positive aspects of this great law and all of its mysterious wonders. Perhaps this is the beginning of a greater plan. Linda Dix, a respected Tarot Reader in Toledo, told Frenchie of a unique change. Perhaps this is just the tip of the iceberg. "It is so nice to wake up with a more positive attitude that I have acquired since Psychic Sunday when this whole transformation entered the embryonic stage. **"I must also admit that with the change of my attitude, I have changed my habits and my health has improved also,"** Frenchie concluded. **"Thanks to my increased faith and renewed spirit, did something positive enough to warrant a complete transformation in my life."**

# A DEADLY FIREY MESSAGE FROM THE GRAVE

In a small town in Tennessee, a farming family came into an unexpected insurance settlement as a result of the death of a distant relative. The family consisted of the farmer, his wife, two teenage daughters and the wife of his son who gave the ultimate sacrifice in Viet Nam. Neither of the adults could read or write, and the children were fortunate to be able to count to ten. The only literate person in the house was the wife of the deceased veteran. Since his death, his wife, Mary, had come to Tennessee to live with her in-laws. Mary was accustomed to getting her way prior to her husband's death. She was really a greedy woman who would stop at nothing to get what she wants.

After the, inheritance, their first purchase was a new suit of clothes for everyone. The second item was a car. No one had a license to drive but that was no deterrent. The day after the purchase of the car, the old man wrecked the car, and he was found behind the wheel of a car almost completely wrapped around an old oak tree. The smell of local mountain distilled alcohol filled the air. It was decided that the old man was drunk and had a gallon of home squeezing in the vehicle. It was common knowledge that the only time the old man would take a nip was at a wedding, or for medicinal purposes with a little rock candy or perhaps a sprig of mint as a cough syrup. On the farm, alcohol was not used except as a medicine and there was never any overindulgence.

The next few days, the old two story house seemed amazingly empty, as the head chair at the dinner table sat quietly as the rest of the family struggled to complete even the most basic of meals.

The two daughters knew that their sister-in-law had been caught a number if times with a bottle of the local brew. She had even been caught totally inebriated and a couple of times, passed out in the barn. They suspected that she had some involvement in the death of their father, but could not put a finger on it. They secretly kept an eye on the sister-in-law for weeks afterward, in the hopes of discovering some clue as to the actual truth behind the death of their father.

In less than a month, tragedy struck the still mourning family with an unexplained fire that started in the upper floor of the house. Again, death took its toll on the mother of the family. She was found near the stairs, and a strong aroma of whiskey emanated from her asphyxiated body. She too, had suffered the same unexplained fate as her husband. After her removal from the burned out building, the sister-in-law presented a will that she had supposedly discovered just prior to the fire. The girls did not know what the will meant, but they soon learned. It appeared that the old man had prepared a will making his son's wife the executrix of his estate. The signature of the old man was simply the usual mark of any Tennessee illiterate, the "x." It was witnessed by an illegible signature, but remained unquestioned by the local officials.

It was almost a week before the family and the sister-in-law returned to the burned out shell. The stairwell upstairs was rickety but the daughters decided to traverse it. Upon entering the mother's bedroom, the elder daughter let out a blood-curdling scream. The second sister came running in. On the one remaining badly burned, smoked wall, where the water had caused the smoke damage to run, there appeared in clear sight the perfectly clear image of their sister-in-law holding a jug of moonshine in one hand and a torch in the other. The sisters did not know how to explain this phenomenon, but it definitely confirmed their suspicions about their sister-in-law being behind the death of both parents. The scream brought the sister-in-law running in from the barn for where she had made a dash as soon as they arrived back on the farm.

The sister-in-law flew up the rickety stairs into the room and froze as she saw the picture depicting her as the cause of the two deaths. She turned to the two sisters and screamed her innocence. "This is a trick," she screamed. "I didn't do it." The two sisters looked at the smoke drawing again and gasped. This time, the picture depicted the two parents as alive, one on each side of the sister-in-law. The sister-in-law was apparently engulfed in flames. As they gazed into the faces of their parents, the floor gave way, dropping the sister-in-law to the floor below. She fell on a gallon of moonshine and suddenly burst into flames. The sisters looked at the smoked drawing again, and it was no longer distinguishable. They ran down the stairs in an attempt to escape the renewed fire, which was rapidly consuming the rest of the building.

The daughters ran to the barn to hitch up the buggy to go for help. As they climbed into the buggy, a bag dislodged under the seat containing the entire inheritance, in cash, that had caused two undeserved deaths and the "eye for an eye" that is still prevalent in many Appalachian areas today.

# PSYCHOMETRY

## The Art of Touch

A great number of people possess the gift of psychometry but don't understand the impressions or how to interpret the various sensations that come with the "reading" of an object.

Psychometry has become more accepted and appreciated the past few decades. People are beginning to appreciate the benefits derived from a good psychometrist.

Psychometry is the art of discovering the character and influence of a person, place or thing, and discovering the surroundings and/or actions involved. It can easily be performed by holding an object, coming in contact with someone, or entering a room charged with the vibrations of the person to be psychometrized. In many cases, the results come immediately. With others, it may take more time, study, and meditation. The impressions usually come in hunches. Other times, you may actually "see" a person. You might hear, smell, or feel impressions that help to interpret a message.

It's called *"programming."* You are actually sending (conscious or unconscious) messages to the brain producing positive or negative results. Next time you tell someone that you have an ailment, remember, *"Thoughts are things."* In the same respect that a thought is a thing, also remember that thoughts have wings. In many cases, the same thoughts that cause an ailment, while transmitting to the brain, often transfer to the brain of someone else. Not always is the message interpreted or recognized, but it's there. How many times has someone given you a most serious excuse not to do something? You knew they were lying through their teeth. Take a few minutes to think about this.

Numerous healing techniques exist. Regardless of the method employed, have your own body and mind in harmony before taking the first step. Jesus, a great psychic and healer, was always in tune with the universal mind consciousness or God consciousness. Set your thoughts in order. Take a few moments in a secluded place and tell yourself what you earnestly believe about life and the Godhead. Many religious leaders will tell you that hell is a burning fire; others say it is in your heart. Still others are convinced that we are serving hell on earth, and death is heaven, true bliss.

Empty your mind of all garbage, all negative thoughts and ill will against everyone. You may have convictions that you don't want to admit. Acknowledge them. Healings, whether done on someone else, or on you, are not done for praise or money. Consider it a star in your crown, a crown that only you can see. Remember, "Like attracts like." You are the architect of your own constellation; one of which the majority of is your own inner being.

I began visiting the various churches. Consider Baptist, Methodist, Mormon, and others, comparing healing techniques. I always felt that everyone could be a healer because the bible says, "Physician, heal thyself." One only has to recognize that he is but a channel for healing through the universal consciousness. This consciousness is linked to the soul of all mankind. Look for this union and recognize the power within yourself, and accept and transmit the energy readily available to you. I have respect for any sincere healer, regardless of the methods he employs. As a church member has faith in God, or a higher being, he also places his trust in the minister who teaches him. If either factor is absent, one less seat would fill the pews.

Man uses less than 10% of his brain capacity. As most ailments are "self inflicted," why can "self" not cure those same illnesses? The need for sickness is often the inner consciousness carrying out a subliminal plan for the end result of a preconceived act. If you are scheduled to give a lecture and are unprepared, why not develop a sore throat or headache? How many children get sick in school and are perfectly normal upon arriving back at home? The complex organ we call the mind does not know if we are actually sick or subconsciously sending thoughts to the brain that we are physically ill. The majority of ailments disappear as soon as the cause is dissolved. Have you ever developed a headache when you had company, only to find it goes as soon as your guests have left? Have you ever been on a date and said you had a headache, to find moments later that you "actually" have one?

Psychometry is not only an art that can be practiced by those having normal sight. It can be performed by sightless individuals as well. I have received messages from people who have been blind from five to fifteen years. In most cases, they had not heard of psychometry until they lost their sight. I had the opportunity to attend a workshop with a nationally known psychic, Carol Ann Liaros who had been working with the blind in New York. This remarkable woman is truly a gifted psychic who has achieved tremendous success in teaching the blind to see utilizing the art of psychometry. According to Ms. Liaros, blind people tend to be more psychic than people with normal vision, as that is their only sense of sight. This leads to the conclusion that there is a connection between the brain and nervous system that connects to the finger tips.

It is possible to become extremely proficient at psychometry after only a few hours of training. If you are not satisfied with your progress, don't give up. Persistence is the key to success. Read, study and meditate.

The sense of touch and receptivity should be well developed in both hands. Yet, I have found that if a person is right handed, his receptivity is often better in his left hand. This is not always the case. Experiment with both hands. If neither seems to be better, place the item to your forehead, close your eyes and try again. Many people work with their eyes open. I work much better with my eyes closed.

Psychometry, like any art or craft, can be developed as anything else through proper training. If no teacher is available and you decide to go it on your own, you must set up a regular ritual. Collect a few small items such as old letters from the attic, rings, pictures and anything else readily available. If you do not have a regular meditation period or have never meditated before, you will probably find your mind cluttered with problems of the day. I have found that to count down from 100 to 0 is most effective.

Grete Grammar, a noted Dutch psychic suggests selecting a "mantra." A mantra is a word or group of words which you find soothing; and through repetitious chanting, sooths the body and calms the mind. You will find her book *PSYCHIC MEDITATION* very helpful. (This book is probably out of print and might be hard to locate.) Her book was easy to read and understand. It was written for the everyday student and the neophyte. The use of either of these techniques will occupy your mind, and your mind will tire and become bored with the task. This will eliminate problems that hamper success. After meditation, select an article and "feel" the vibrations. The method in which you hold the object to be psychometrized is up to you. Try holding small items in your fist. In the case of rings, place it on your finger and rub it with your thumb. After trying different techniques, decide which seems easier for you. Rubbing your fingertips across articles like photographs, sealed envelopes, etc. might prove to be of greater value.

# GROWTH
## Physically, Emotionally, Spiritually

As we measure the inches we add to our structure, we are also aware of our emotional growth. We are continually aware of the ups and downs that cause grief in our everyday life. What we often fail to recognize is our spiritual growth. With this in mind, we must first construct a pattern to adhere to in this monumental task. During our earliest years, we are more cognizant of our spirituality than when we reach our teens and abandon our spirituality. It seems at this point that spiritual growth takes back burner in our life, and we tend to completely dismiss this from our life. There is usually a mesa that we must mount before we can face the fact that we have abandoned the most important aspect of our growth. Whether we are a religious scholar or atheist, the fact remains that we have a spiritual ladder that we have to climb to complete our physical and spiritual growth. Once we have achieved our spiritual enlightenment, our emotional growth will take care of itself. This is the latter of the three phases in our growth. The first two must be completed and the third will take care of itself. The latter is of less consequence than the first two.

The power of the most high spiritual entity can come upon you and it "shall" happen. The most famous psychic/healer/prophet has said, "As you believe, so shall you become. With God, all things are possible." Whether the belief is in God, Buddha, or Allah, the result is still the same.

If your belief is strong and unfaltering, that in which you believe with all your spirit is possible. The Great Spirit plants seeds of growth within each of us. This is relevant as most of us at this point allow the weeds of negativity to creep in and destroy our newly acquired faith. As the seeds of positive aspirations grow, the weeds grow immeasurably. Why should we have such a small vision of faith in the Great Spirit? Regardless of our faith, most of us believe in the creation of the universe being the direct result of "some" higher intelligence.

The wild weeds that creep into our psyche are a direct result of the "small-minded mentality" that so many of us seem to adopt in our daily routine. Why think of a fifty-cent raise at our job when we should think about owning the company.

This is a hypothetical example: The king of Saudi Arabia invited Arnold Palmer to his country for golf lessons. During his stay, Arnold was treated to only the finest luxuries anywhere. Upon his departure, the king asked Arnold what he would like as a parting gift. Arnold said his trip was sufficient and no payment was necessary. The king insisted on giving Arnold some type of "thank you" gift. Finally, realizing that the king would win, Arnold said, "I would like a new golf club." The next few weeks, Arnold kept checking his mail expecting a golf club in the mail. What would it be like? Would it be embedded with diamonds and precious stones? Finally, a few days later, Arnold was surprised to get a small envelope in the mail.

He couldn't imagine what it could be since he knew it was not a new golf club. Much to his surprise, the envelope contained a deed for a NEW GOLF CLUB *AND RESORT* in a nearby city.

One who lives in a small one-room efficiency apartment might conceivably wish for a larger apartment. A person who is climbing the ladder of spiritual growth and inspiration would go one step farther and wish for a new home. The seeds that grow to accomplish this task must be guarded against the weeds that will smother all hopes of achievement. If we're going to receive anything, we have to have that vision inside. We must go beyond the thoughts and seeds of the past. We must conquer the weeds that hamper our growth. The determining factor is to keep the power of a higher spirit guiding us on the path of life. We must recognize our guardian angels or spirit guides, and allow them to be our guide and assist us with the map placed before us. We need to recognize the spiritual insight in order to determine which road we want to take.

Now is the time to wash our negative thinking down the drain. Now is the time to wash all negative thoughts about our neighbors and to say only good things about them. Now is the time to dispel all ill will. Negative thoughts and comments about our neighbors are returned to us three fold. If we say ill about our neighbor or a coworker to our friends, do they think better of us? What they think about us is the fact that we gossip and harbor the weeds of spiritual destruction. Our friends don't think better of us by our gossip. In most cases, they don't even want to hear it.

Those to whom we pass on negativity do not bring us more friends or praise. It merely causes a gray shadow to be cast upon us. As we cast aspersions on our neighbors, we are inviting it to return to us three fold. The law of three is invoked with every statement we make, with each thought we think. A thought is a thing although it cannot be measured. What goes from us returns to us. It is up to us to make it be a blessing or a curse.

Begin each day with a prayer and thanks for that which we have received and for that which
## *We have yet to receive!*

# ANCIENT LADY DEFIES TORNADO

The Lady of Crete, forged from molten lava over 400 years ago, gained national attention when her story appeared in FATE® Magazine in 2005, after she donned her death mask in 1971.

Her earthen brown colors remain vibrant as long as the path of her protector is safe. In the event of imminent danger, her brown hue is gradually replaced by a gray death mask.

According to legend, the Lady is an ancient protector and guardian of the dead. In addition to guarding and directing the departed soul to a higher level, she acts as a centurion to guard and protect her owner. It is a common belief that disaster will befall anyone who steals her or owns her through any monetary transaction. She can be passed on lovingly from one person to another. If her current owner dies she becomes the guardian of the nearest relative in the household. She was given to me by a friend who died of cancer. Since her story appeared in FATE® dozens of calls have come into my office with outlandish offers to buy her.

In 1971, the office where she stood vigil was seriously damaged by fire. The one room embracing her gaze sustained no damage.

Everyone dreams of spending their golden years in paradise away from the trials and tribulations of everyday life. We expect to live way into our golden years without pain or woes. We expect to be healthy enough to mow the lawn at 80. Some of us expect to live in a community where our lawn is mowed for us.

These are the plans that I had harbored for years until my brother and business partner in a printing shop in the Historical Polish Village in Toledo, suffered his first heart attack resulting in a two way bypass. From that time on, it seems that life had dealt us a bad hand of cards. Lyle was just getting back on his feet when I went to the dentist with a toothache. The dentist reluctantly told he suspected throat cancer to be the source of my discomfort. After three other opinions, I was admitted to Toledo Hospital.

I had just begun my recovery after radiation and all the misery that accompanied it, when Lyle went back into the hospital for a 4 way bypass.

Operating the business became more and more difficult as the days went on. Business was failing because of the economy, unheard of utility bills ranging over $1,000 a month with no relief in sight. I prayed for the days of President Clinton to return when at least we could afford to put bread on the table. Now our food money went to pay utilities, gas for the car, insurance and soaring taxes.

On February 2, 2006, I retired and bought a new home in Florida.

My brother suffered a massive heart attack only minutes from Toledo, Ohio. The doctor said he wouldn't last an hour. Five days later after Lyle went into the "step-down" unit, I proceeded to Florida with the furniture. I returned to Toledo to make plans for a carefully executed trip to take him home. The temperature was $9^0$ below zero. I waited for warmer weather to assure a more comfortable trip. A rough trip could prove fatal.

On March 1, 2006, my birthday, we arrived at our retirement home. During Lyle's hospital stay, my truck was parked in a mall parking lot in Bowling Green, Ohio. As I unloaded the truck, I discovered that thieves had helped themselves. Dozens of boxes were taken. I was relieved to discover the Lady of Crete had not been touched. She was the best packed and most accessible. Her crate had been opened and the packing removed. I could feel her glow as I placed her on her pedestal where she has watched over me for over half a century. I often wonder what ill fate befell the thieves.

I lived the American Dream until early February 2, 2007 when a tornado, equivalent to category 5 hurricanes, ripped through DeLand with only moment's notice. I heard the famous "train sound" seconds before the roof blew off the house. I helped Lyle get into my van as it became airborne. Miraculously my roof came back down on top of the van hurling us back down to earth.

We fought our way out of the mangled van to observe an almost vacant lot with only one room standing. The door opened easily and everything was in pristine condition. The Lady of Crete grimly displayed her second "death mask" in over fifty years.

The gated retirement community of over 280 homes was reduced by almost half. A street sign from Daytona Beach, over 30 miles away, was planted in my front yard. Outside the house next door lay a bathtub, causing one to have second thoughts about that being one of the safest places to hide.

As morning broke, the fire department was on the scene with search and rescue. The Red Cross and Salvation Army came in to supply food and fresh water.

My neighbors across the street got into their car in an attempt to seek shelter. A tree broke off at the base and went through their windshield separating the two. Horror and disbelief was beginning to set-in. What had been a peaceful retirement community was no-more.

With no help from FEMA and little help from insurance, I managed to find a new home. On February 2, 2006, I bought my first new home. On February 2, 2007, it was totally destroyed by the tornado.

On March 1, 2006, I moved into my first new home. On March 1, 2007, I moved into my second retirement home.

After rising to almost roof level and being hurled back to earth, neither of us sustained as much as a scratch. Karma, or just bit chin' bad luck? This is a story that should not and could not have happened...
**But it did!**

# TRAPPINGS OF A PSYCHIC VAMPIRE

Jhanina came to the United States from Transylvania, in 1917. She was an inspired young girl destined to make her mark in America. She walked the cold streets of Cleveland, Ohio seeking any means of livelihood available.

She arrived at the sponsorship of a greedy aunt who had only ideas of claiming a portion of any funds that Jhanina may earn. "If you don't pay your way and help with the bills," she constantly nagged, "I will send you back home." This only angered Jhanina and made her ever more determined to find work. She walked the streets day and night until she found a job as a nanny with a prominent doctor at the Cleveland Clinic. She reveled at the prospect of making twenty-five cents a day.

It was only a few weeks before she enrolled in a nursing school in Cleveland. She quickly advanced to the top of her class in both practice and ethics. She was sought after by some of the most prominent physicians and surgeons in the state. Her patients included the Shaw of Iran as well as many governors and noted Ohio politicians. In her entire nursing career, she never had a patient succumb to their illness. I asked her secret. She told me that she only loaned them her healing energy. If she ever got sick and needed the energy, she could take it back.

Once she began making a normal salary, her aunt demanded half. Refusing to comply, Jhanina moved out on her own, fell in love and married to a prominent Cleveland businessman. She set up homemaking in Clyde, Ohio and buried her husband in 1966.

I met Jhanina at a spiritual retreat in Toledo, Ohio in 1966. She was seeking the assistance of a healing psychic. Claiming to be the victim of a psychic vampire, she felt she was under the influence of some evil force. "I know who it is," she sobbed. "It is my neighbor whom I spurned when he asked me to have an affair."

I was young, naïve and decent looking. I had absolutely no clue as to whose will I was being drawn. Jhanina's husband had just passed away after a decade of fighting cancer. "The doctor gave him six months. I *'babied'* him for ten long years after that," she said boastfully. I suppose it was the burial of her husband that caused her to become more demanding. She was a healer whose purpose was to heal. Now she was the one who needed healing.

Television was continually showing re-runs of vampires with many classic actors that we have learned to love and hate. This vampire is a different species. This vampire does not suck the blood out of you causing you to live forever; he sucks the life giving energy out of you. History records many cases of vampirism which are active in our hidden society today. This "new to the market" vampire is a lecherous villain that can be a friend, family member or someone we meet on the street. The most loved and refined grandmother or grandfather can be among those falling under this spell.

Our closest friend is often the most vicious to fall into this category. These are the worst kind. There is no remorse. The most minute spark of concern from a friend who is attempting to drain your energy can appear to be a closely dedicated friend who offers you total support and strength while harboring the motive of draining your energy.

I often awoke after a recuperative night's sleep feeling positive about a new day, but somehow had a foreboding feeling hovering over me. I began to feel depleted of my energy and accomplished little during the day. If I was already suffering from any affliction, this feeling was compounded.

Psychics described my aura and expressed concern of a drain on my energy. It was a difficult situation to overcome after the initial shock of learning of the attack of a psychic vampire. If I was not mentally prepared to warrant off such an attack, the psychic vampire had a joyous day without any fear of retaliation.

The number of psychic vampires is countless. Many don't realize they drain the energy from those around them. This person can be sitting by you in church, on the bus or the taxi driver.

A jealous psychic vampire is among the most vicious. The amount of greed, jealousy and hate they harbor adds to the power of their vengeance. They make it a policy to consciously zap their target every chance they get.

The most important tool we have to combat psychic vampires is simply the knowledge that they do exist. I was psychically and mentally protecting myself through concentration, meditation and prayer to improve my odds of winning.

I remember allowing Jhanina to visit me at my home near Bowling Green, Ohio. She arrived with an extreme case of infected edema in her right leg. She stayed with me for almost a week receiving healing energy and prayer on a daily basis. Her outlook on religion was somewhat dismal and leaned toward the occult. I paid no attention to her rambling about a vicious circle of men and women who projected evil toward her. This was simply dismissed as the rambling of an ill informed, deranged, middle aged dowager. I agreed with everything she said as I knew I would have to resort to her level of thinking in order to affect any healing what-so-ever. I acted as though I knew everything about the "demons" she seemed to be running from. "They come for me from every direction" she commented, "especially at night when I am trying to sleep."

It was shortly after her visit that I seemed to lose interest in everyday occurrences, experience a loss of appetite, and just felt all around drained. This lack of energy continued for the next couple of weeks. Finally, after a myriad of attempts to regain my strength, I submitted to a physical. The results were about what I expected; nothing wrong. "Over exertion and lack of sleep" was the doctor's non committal response. He suggested a multi-vitamin on a daily basis. I always ate healthy and a vitamin was the last thing I needed.

A week later I was in the hospital with pneumonia. Jhanina heard about my illness and rushed to my bedside as though she expected it. I was discharged to recuperate at home with a prescription for six pills on a regular basis. Jhanina subjected me to a variety of healing techniques from incense surrounding my head to anointing me with oil and sprinkling sage around my bed. My recovery was remarkable and seemed to take no time at all.

A month later I visited the dentist with a toothache. The dentist looked at me somewhat puzzled as I was there only two weeks prior and given a clean bill of health. He examined me more closely. "I don't know how to tell you this," he said, "I think you have throat cancer." After the initial shock, I sought a second opinion and a third and fourth. I could not believe they all told me the same thing.

I was admitted to Toledo Hospital where I underwent extensive laser surgery removing most of my bottom gum, a tonsil and part of my tongue. Again, Jhanina came to my rescue after my discharge from the hospital. She stayed with me and nursed me back to health.

In a matter of weeks, I became ill again. It appeared that my pneumonia had returned with a vengeance. Before I could pick up the phone to make an appointment with my doctor, Jhanina was at the door. "I will take care of you," she said. She immediately began making a mustard plaster, popular in the late 1800's and early 1900's. A vaporizer was placed by my bed with salty water emitting a steady stream of moisture. A rub with Vicks was an hourly ritual. Soon, I was back to normal again. There was no explanation for my sudden attack of serious illnesses.

Without realizing that I was falling deeper into the clutches of a professional manipulator, I continued to accept the healing energy that she so freely offered. This continued for months before the situation took on a new direction. Now, it is Jhanina who needs attention. Her obsession with the dark forces that had plagued her for years now reared their ugly heads. Now, Jhanina is the one needing constant attention.

Since she had come to my aid on many occasions, I felt compelled to reciprocate. For weeks I took the tedious 265-mile trip from my home to Clyde, Ohio. Sometimes I was so tired that she offered me the sofa to spend the night. I worked on her many ailments, some visible, some imaginary, for hours on end. The daily trips were starting to take a toll on me financially. The gas, car maintenance, toll fees had already reached far in excess of the thousand-dollar mark. "Don't worry," she said. "I will take care of the bill." She began giving me ten dollars each time I arrived. The ten dollars did not cover the expense one way. After the many trips she made to care for me, how could I place a dollar value on my concern?

After six months of daily trips to Clyde, I decided, "enough is enough." I told her this is my last trip. My finances won't stand further trips and my nerves certainly won't. "You don't have to come up every day," she said, "a couple of times a week is enough." I tried to convince her that this was my last time. "You can send me healing energy from home," she said. "All you have to do is '*think about it*,' and it will be done." I told her that I would send her healing thoughts and prayers from home. "A prayer won't do it," she screamed, "this is black magic and it needs black magic to fight it!" She reminded me how she had always come to my rescue when I was sick and I owed her the same respect. The trips she made to my home were less than a dozen. I had already made almost 200 trips to Clyde.

Her phone calls plagued me on a daily basis through half the night. Finally, I had my phone number changed. She sent a private investigator to my shop. He purchased a couple of office supplies and asked for a receipt. I promptly obliged. He asked if it had my correct phone number for telephone orders. I assured him that the number was correct.

The next day my phone at work began ringing off the hook. She had succeeded in finding my work number and the turmoil started over again. There seemed to be no place I could turn to avoid her chiding and insensitive phone calls. Finally, in desperation, I decided to close the business and move to Florida. I took an early retirement and hoped to escape the annoying calls of the worst acquaintance I had ever made in my life.

I moved to Florida on February 2, 2006. It wasn't long before she found me. The calls continued to come in on a daily basis. She kept telling me that I owed her my full attention to help her overcome her evil spell. I made two trips to Clyde after my relocation. She told me that unless I continued to protect her from the evil eye, it would fall on my shoulders. The ranting became progressively more threatening. "You owe me," she continually shouted. I tried to convince her to go into assisted living. She would not even consider the idea. "You can come up every other week and pick up my supplies," she ordered! "I don't need anyone else." My last trip to Clyde was in January, 2007. I returned on February 2, 2007, the day a category five tornado ripped through my retirement community, totally demolishing my new home. The only room left standing was my sanctuary which housed the ***LADY OF CRETE,*** an ancient protector which I had inherited about the same time that my ordeal began.

By this time, she was confined permanently to a wheel chair. She needed someone. She demanded that someone, visit her on a daily basis to help her take care of personal hygiene.
She contacted an attorney and appointed me as her power of attorney. I began receiving nuisance calls from her physician as to why I am abusing a senior citizen.

In October 2007, she called ordering me to bring her a new microwave. I bought a new one but shipped it through a mailing service in DeLand.

Later, in October 2007, she called again and ordered that I take care of her funeral arrangements. She sent me a photo of her tombstone bearing the name of her husband as well as her own. Her husband died over 50 years ago. Under her name was her birth of 1906-19__. The stone will have to be reworked to reflect the new century, 2007.

After almost 50 years of trial and tribulation, I realize the most popular tool of choice is simple reverse psychology. It is the best way to get what you want and make the victim willing to do your bidding. This is a lesson boldly learned and well deserved and will never be forgotten.

Realizing the presence of the harborage of negativity of those with whom we come in contact is only half the battle. The other half of the battle is to resist being a victim and become a victor.

In late October 2007, I made a final trip to Clyde. I went to oversee the funeral arrangements and make sure she was buried beside her beloved husband; thus ending almost a 50 year ordeal of psychic domination. The tombstone was repaired and engraved. There were no mourners. I made sure there were enough flowers to give the appearance that she was loved and respected by all.

Look for one of these stories to be the plot of a movie.
Thank you for 50 years of support.
Charlie R. Brown
www.bodymindspiritnews.com

www.ingramcontent.com/pod-product-compliance
Lightning Source LLC
Chambersburg PA
CBHW020010050426
42450CB00005B/401